An Artist in Java
and Other Islands of Indonesia

D1558212

An Artist in Java
and Other Islands of Indonesia

By
Jan Poortenaar

Translated from the Dutch
by Horace Shipp
in collaboration with the Author

With a Foreword by Frank Brangwyn, R. A.

SINGAPORE
OXFORD UNIVERSITY PRESS
OXFORD   NEW YORK

Oxford University Press

Oxford New York Toronto
Delhi Bombay Calcutta Madras Karachi
Petaling Jaya Singapore Hong Kong Tokyo
Nairobi Dar es Salaam Cape Town
Melbourne Auckland
and associated companies in
Berlin Ibadan

Oxford is a trade mark of Oxford University Press

Originally published as An Artist in the Tropics *by Sampson Low,*
Marston & Co., Ltd. London, c.1928

First issued as an Oxford University Press paperback 1989
Second impression 1990

ISBN 0 19 588950 9

Printed in Malaysia by Peter Chong Printers Sdn. Bhd.
Published by Oxford University Press Pte. Ltd.,
Unit 221, Ubi Avenue 4, Singapore 1440

Foreword

DESPITE all that is said to the contrary, we artists find as much joy in looking at each other's work as in the creation of our own, and in appreciating the individual vision and technical achievement of men whose painting may differ from ours. It is in that spirit that I give my blessing to Jan Poortenaar's book. It commends itself to me from more than one angle: firstly, as might be anticipated, from that of my admiration of Mr. Poortenaar's drawings and paintings, which are reproduced; secondly, because the whole scheme of taking an " art journey " with pencil and brush and a mind alert for effects, to so fascinating a place as Java, could not but bring interesting results; and, again, because he has, through his highly-placed introductions, given us a glimpse into phases of Javanese life which are seldom open to the European visitor.

Thus this pleasant book, which is other than an art book, other than a travel book, other than a log. Naturally, as an artist, I am chiefly concerned with the author's visualisation of the strange and beautiful, and often terrible, country, and of the exquisite dramatic life which he found there. I have long been interested in the development of Jan Poortenaar's art, and in the exotic life of the Malay Archipelago he seems to me to have found a subject eminently suited to his individual sense of design and decorative interpretation. In the hope that others will become better acquainted with his work through this volume, I sign myself as its god-parent.

FRANK BRANGWYN.

Translator's Introduction

PERHAPS that is very wrong and misleading, for in truth I am only one half or less than one half the translator, unless I can claim to have translated from the very original English into which Jan Poortenaar and his wife first rendered the book from their own Dutch. Now and again a particularly exotic turn of phrase would cause me to delve at first hand into *Een Kunstreis in de Tropen*, with the aid of a Dutch dictionary, but mainly my task has been to find English proper for English unconfined by rules of grammar or syntax. Obviously I was handicapped, for the authors' licence was a hundred times more expressive than the translator's pedantry. They would talk of a " monkey-folded-up man", and I would cover a sheet of paper experimenting for a phrase which kept their figure and succintness. If I share at all the honour of this book it is that I have been faithful to their mood and manner. As the manuscript came to my hand it had a freedom from formality which gave it an individual charm. Now descriptive, sensuous, and visual as only an artist would make it; now informative, now humorous, its quick changes of direction demanded changes in the quality and tempo of the prose. Otherwise it became a different book; and that means the translator turned transplanter. Often the prose is so shot through with emotion as to verge upon the domains of poetry, and, at the risk of being charged with flamboyance, I have remained faithful to the mood of those passages.

Jan Poortenaar and his wife are, before all else, artists in form and colour and sound; the book they have written bears the impress of that.

Translator's Introduction

One other word must in justice be added, and that a gesture towards the " Shadowy Third " in our collaboration. Geertruida van Vladeracken-Poortenaar's place is by rights upon the title-page of this book. Not only for the reason that the concert tour which formed a basis of the journey was primarily hers, but that she actually was part author, part translator, and certainly inspirer of this book.

HORACE SHIPP.

Contents

Contents

List of Illustrations

List of Illustrations

An Artist in the Tropics

Chapter One

Comforters and Guides

WHEN first we conceived the plan of spending an undefined period in that "Somewhere East of Suez" where the tropical East stretches an arm of land three thousand miles long towards Australia, we did it with the light-hearted cheerfulness of enthusiasts. We loved travel, and here were strange sights and stranger peoples, other skies, other men, other manners; we loved the arts, and here we could practise music and painting and literature, my wife, Geertruida van Vladeracken, giving concerts as we went, I filling sketch-books, and both of us concocting this book of our impressions. We should be brought into touch, moreover, with the surviving native art of these vast islands, and in particular with the exquisite theatre art of the Wayang and of the Court dancing which had already attracted the attention of European theatre lovers by its tradition of exotic beauty. So it was to be an art journey through the Eastern Tropics, a quest of beauty and interest, with some little air of the Troubadour about it; for had we not songs for sale?

But the mooting of our project brought about us a multitude of counsellors. Warnings, advice, exhortations, experiences, threats, poured upon us; always with the moral that "East is East and West is West, and never the twain shall meet." Travel it seemed, at least travel with safety to body and estate, ended where *Le Train Bleu* came to a standstill, or might be extended in the season to Cairo without immediate fear of disaster or assassination. It was

An Artist in the Tropics

hinted that if by chance we returned from our *terra incognita* with our lives, the extreme discomforts of our various experiences would, on many occasions, make mere annihilation a welcome choice. Evidently one could not go to the East in any irresponsible manner.

"You couldn't wear black boots out there, nor a rubber raincoat, I assure you. Both are much too hot."

So the chapter of warnings opened upon us. Almost guiltily we abandoned these articles. We were young then in this matter of advice; we even made solemn little notes of it. Arrived in the East itself, and before proceeding up-country, the torrent thickened. Sometimes we even sought an opinion, as for example, when we questioned whether it would be advisable to keep money under the pillow at night.

"That's no use," our counsellor disconcertingly informed us. "They simply blow some narcotic into your room and dope you. Easily done, because doors and windows all have lattice work. Thus they can rob you of everything without your even waking. And don't hang those native daggers or krisses to ornament your walls. That is most dangerous. If a burglar does break in your own weapon may. . . . "

"*Doux pays.*"

"And never drink tea out of the old bronze or brass pots. In the old days they were used to prepare poison, and you never can tell."

So our comforters reassured us. In the Indies one likes a truly Oriental story of hidden forces, mystical influences and so forth, and evidently we were not to be disappointed. We returned to the practical subject of the safety of our money only to face another disquieting possibility.

"At least you must not carry it in your pockets. In the crowds one cut with a sharp knife through your linen suit—and gone is your wallet."

Looking back upon those counsels for our safety, and remembering that we covered distances as great as from Scotland to Asia Minor and from Marseille to Moscow, we conclude that most of our advisors are Oriental in the fantasy of their imaginations. Especially in the hotels, we learned, must we be on guard. Nevertheless we came back alive; not once were we drugged, nor poisoned, nor even stabbed, although we consistently omitted to lock our doors.

A PALM TREE *(Drawing)*

Comforters and Guides

Neither were we robbed, and nothing disappeared from our unlocked trunks and wardrobes—a record for honesty which vies with the best in European travel.

Alongside the robbery-with-subtle-violence myth stand the danger-from-disease stories, and the less threatening matter of essential luggage.

"Thirty-six white suits you will need."

We gasp, contemplating the ever-growing list of necessities, and plead to be allowed to experiment with six.

"Canvas for painting?"

"Take it with you!" This with much firmness. "If you find any there at all it is as bad as it is expensive."

This at least proved to be sound advice. A shopkeeper in Medan cheerfully asked over £2 a metre for canvas which would cost about four shillings in Europe, and his wares were mouldy and almost perished with damp.

Then:

"Do be extremely careful of even the tiniest scratches. Always carry some crystals of boracic acid. It is safer to make your own lotion for any bandage. Infection can so easily be fatal, and can be contracted in an instant."

"What of water and food?"

"Never drink water even when they call it safe and say that it is boiled. *Aer blanda sadja* (mineral water only) even to brush your teeth."

"Madam," said one fastidious housewife, "I even wash myself with *aer blanda*."

"Be careful that no flies touch your food. If one leaves one's house for a journey and stays at a small hotel or Government guest-house, those of us who know the country always order toast, thoroughly hot toast. The toasting disinfects the food, and so long as it is hot no flies will go near it."

"As we shall be travelling all the time, do we understand that mineral water and toast is all we may have?"

Our informant is aggrieved.

"As you will. I advise you for your good."

"And alcohol?"

"Most doctors agree that a glass of old Dutch gin is the very thing in the East."

An Artist in the Tropics

"Does that also apply to ladies?" we ask.

"Only yesterday somebody told us that the East Indies were a wonderful country, viewed from the comfort of your fireside in Europe on a cold wintry night. Then you can forget the terrible heat, the mosquitoes that sting you everlastingly, and as you contemplate a country where no cold wind howls at your windows you do not remember the glare of the sunlight making everything glow like aluminium in the unbearable heat. And when you turn to alcohol as a remedy, we were told, you rapidly become unbearable yourself, so that your last state is worse than the first."

At which dilemma our mentor turned to a new theme, and gave us strict injunctions as to our intercourse with the natives.

"Never touch a Javanese. He will not forget it until eternity."

"I haven't the slightest intention of doing so," I assured him. "But as a matter of theoretical interest what would actually happen in the circumstances?"

"Your victim would plot with the Kokki,[1] and, without possibility of detection, scrapings of dry bamboo leaves find their way into your food causing an incurable illness."

"Would it be safest to carry a weapon?"

"There is no harm in having one. I always had a revolver under the pillow at night. Not that I ever used it, but the Boy would tell his fellows: 'Boys, my Tuan[2] is no greenhorn,' and they will remember that when they incline to make trouble. I'll show you mine. An ordinary lead bullet will work, but a steel one is better; that will go right through a wall."

And the Browning is taken out of its case.

"Is it loaded?" we ask in a genuine search for information.

"I really don't remember. Now let me see, how *did* the thing work?"

Our friend starts fumbling with the trigger.

"Would you mind turning the barrel in the other direction. There seems such a chance that your excellent steel bullet will go through one of us."

"I beg your pardon. I didn't think of that. I'll hold it vertically."

[1]Kokki : A native cook.   [2]Tuan : Master.

4

Comforters and Guides

We remind our self-appointed East Indian guide that his children are sleeping in the room overhead, and at that moment feel that life in tranquil Holland is sufficiently stimulating, and wonder whether the Indies can surpass it. At least we were prepared for anything to happen in the vast, wild places of that eerie country.

Chapter Two

Travelling Companions

TRAVELLING may be accomplished in two ways. Either one is the respectable tourist, a *grand seigneur*, a cosmopolitan, attended by waiters, chamber-maids, boot-boys and queued-up porters as one leaves each hotel; or one is plebeian, travelling almost without aid outside himself, carrying large portions of his own luggage like a tramp, and shrugging scornful shoulders at Pullman-cars and de-luxe expresses. Either manner has its advantages, but they cannot be combined. The former method keeps you in a drawing-room atmosphere, with boots exquisitely polished and evening dress close to hand, but against this the surroundings tend to lack character; the latter may lack comfort, but it will never lack experience or variety.

Ocean travel is the same as land travel in these matters. The mail steamers share with the great hotels their cosmopolitan uniformity. Their passengers all wear a dinner jacket of the same cut, and screen all their feelings, emotions and personalities behind a politeness equally uniform. Conversations never flag but they never pass beyond the superficialities, whilst the polished talkers pursue their own real thoughts into the hinterlands of their minds. "*Le monde où l'on s'ennuie.*" Of these steamers little else can be related other than the elaborateness of the dinners, the excellence of the service, the progress of bridge parties or deck sports. On the smaller boats these fashionable matters may have little place, but their loss is amply compensated for by the glimpses into men's minds, the camaraderie with real people.

Thus we travelled. Our steamer carried cargo, and a fascinating conglomeration of characters among its thirty passengers. We had not calculated upon that, but knew only that our purse had decreed that the journey must not be made in *grand seigneur* fashion.

6

RICEFIELDS *(Etching)*

Travelling Companions

Until one is actually on the seas bound for some remote part of the world for some unlimited period the thousand and one preparations form a futurist nightmare in the mind. It whirls kaleidoscopically, demands, decisions and preparations jostling each other in frantic haste; then suddenly the last trunk is closed, the last thing done, and a sudden void, as though magic has put an end to this hectic existence of getting ready. Nothing more is left to organise nor to think about, and the next morning we jog in dreamy reaction down to the East India docks.

Our special little train carries us past no end of sheds, cranes, boats, and wharves, but at last we alight with our steamer towering above us. Already the East meets us, for a crowd of Chinese stand ready to deal with our luggage, and they swarm up the rope ladders like man-apes, and stow our belongings into the cabin. We also bestow ourselves in one of those compact little rooms, where everything so quickly finds its appointed niche. We approve the wardrobe, the table and the settee, the fan and two windows which promise fresh air in plenty. What is this on one of the berths? A *grand-seigneurish* touch—a complimentary letter from Hewitt's Agency who booked our passage wishing us "*bon voyage*". Typically English, we comment, this gracious gesture, and in the meantime—typically English also in its lack of ostentation—the steamer has weighed anchor and luncheon is announced.

We find our seats at one of the five tables, and discover that the majority of the passengers speak English; which means that we are free to talk with them without the embarrassing Dutch custom of introducing oneself formally before a conversation is permissible. Two years in the East Indies is destined to counterbalance this spell of informality, for hardly a day of that time is to pass without the traditional "May I have the pleasure of . . ." since ancient Dutch custom regards anyone as a stranger until this magic formula has been uttered—magic, indeed, for once it is spoken no boundaries seem to be set to inquisitiveness and intrusion.

As everyone who has taken a long sea voyage remembers, this matter of table-companions is one of no small importance, for since it necessitates sitting with them a number of times each day it may become extremely tedious. Two ladies, mother and daughter, the ship's doctor, and two reserved, black-coated gentlemen of ecclesiastical demeanour are our complement. At first sight the

7

An Artist in the Tropics

Chinese servants interest us more than our fellow passengers. The boys wear spotless blue cotton garments, with white starched chemisettes down to the waist, so that we may be forgiven for giving to one who has outstanding serenity of countenance the appellation of "the chorister boy", even though to the prosaically-minded he is number something. The boy at our table is older; he has a wistful, down-on-his-luck expression, reminiscent of the sad, caged monkeys in the Zoo. When, to cheer him, we expressed our pleasure at the toast, it doomed us to toast as long as the journey lasted. A few days after this early encounter someone at another table asked for toast; he came to inspect our store, but finding only two pieces in the toast-rack he steadfastly refused to deprive us of our avowed preference, shook his musing little head with inexpressible sorrow, and shuffled off noiselessly in his soft Chinese slippers to the kitchen.

At one of the near tables a group of young men, still in the cubhood stages of self-importance, issue loud orders to the Chinese boys. What goes on behind those imperturbable masks of faces? One cannot tell, but it is probably more than coincidence that our vociferous young friends have to wait longer than anybody else for the fulfilments of their commands.

The ship's doctor is a wise old bird. He makes good cheer with everybody, but we suspect that he has his own conclusions. The two gentlemen in black are what we should call lay-brothers in Holland; they are bound for the Philippines. The doctor calls them "padre", but it does not save them from his jokes. One of them has sequestered his soul from the world where jokes exist; his fanatic eyes give no sign of what he thinks on such a plane of consciousness. The second, who is called Brother Leo, gradually thaws, and then laughs so gustily that his mirth draws the attention of the neighbouring tables. His face is naturally jolly; it is round and fat, and when he laughs it grows rounder and is good-humour incarnate. But Brother King is silent, no emotion, and certainly no laughter, is permitted to disturb the rigid austerity of his features. Nevertheless he joins the deck games as well as his less severe companion.

Once Brother Leo used his jovial countenance to such good effect that even the immobile Chinese and the impassive Brother King joined into our laughter. The doctor, with the youthful

Travelling Companions

humour which never failed him, had cut a set of grotesque teeth from orange peel and the weird effect which they gave to his debonair appearance excited Brother Leo to emulation. As a grotesque Brother Leo left nothing to be desired. His slightly vacuous face, shaking with his laughter, and adorned with these huge teeth became that of some irrepressibly comic Chinese dragon, and who could wonder that even his brother missioner unbent. The Captain enjoyed the amusement discreetly in the distance; like the good sailor he is, he steers his way pleasantly among his passengers, never running aground upon even the most difficult personality.

Both the Brothers are Irishmen away from their native land for the first time. Ireland is a wonderfully fine country they are agreed; the finest country in the world asserts Brother King, though he has not been to any other. Brother Leo, good-hearted soul that he is, plays enthusiastically all day long with the baby of a young married couple, bo-peeping eternally to its great joy. His love for the child overcomes the obstacle of its unfortunate nationality, for Brother Leo, as Brother King, is a violent Sinn Feiner. We being neutrals, he entreats us with arguments, press cuttings from remote Irish news-sheets, booklets, pamphlets and every other form of propaganda calculated to prove to us the unimpeachable virtue of the cause of Sinn Fein against the unspeakable villainy of everything English.

Before the passengers leave the steamer for the first time a fête is organised. Since it is manifestly impossible for an English steamer to abstain from a fancy dress party, we all try to make ourselves as unrecognisable as possible, and devote the dinner time to penetrating these disguises. A very reserved rubber planter, who has paid practically no attention to his fellow-passengers throughout the voyage, but has confined his attention to the delights of whisky and soda and the card tables, has transformed himself into an amazing counterfeit of Charlie Chaplin. The doctor has sacrificed his moustache to the occasion, and prinks around as a young lady, with manners as bold as the unfading blush on her cheeks or the none-too-delicate outlining of her lashes. Although it is not his accustomed place he seats himself next to Brother King, whose transcendental spirit has made no compromise with these frivolities, and who does not know quite what attitude the spiritual life demands towards such happenings. Brother Leo also is

9

An Artist in the Tropics

metamorphosed into a girl, but one as demure, modest and impeccable as the other is abandoned. At one moment, however, he takes a powder puff from the dainty reticule which dangles from his bare arm and coquettishly powders his nose—to the evident vexation of Brother King, who has now retreated into an enigmatic and Sphinx-like silence.

The Captain has degraded himself to a pirate, with one eye covered with plaster, so that a lady who has hitherto functioned as a fashion plate, in gowns of unimaginable colours and with the vacuity of expression sacred to Society portraits in the illustrated papers, was so horrified that for one moment her well-bred smile dropped off and revealed a genuine expression. It was not until the champagne was poured out that she recovered the soft-as-moonlight smile in its unshaken perfection again. A solemn oriental potentate had evolved from Mr. Banks, an official of the Malay States, who in accordance with his new rôle made an imposing speech to the captain accompanied by equally imposing gestures.

Mr. O'Conner, who had been the driving force of gambling throughout the voyage, alternating "Sweepstakes on the run" with eternal Mah Jongg, appeared as a stout cook; and the whole of the ship's officers were in absurd penny-gaff dresses and made a deafening noise with a Jazz band which drowned even the incessant gramophone when dinner was finished.

It was a break in the monotony of the voyage, that endless monotony punctuated by the padre's soft, Irish voice at my left ear each morning, with its "Nice day, to-day, Mr. Pourtnayr, very nice day," and his luncheon time greeting of "Veery hot to-day; O yeez, O, yeez, veery hot."

The other outstanding memory of the voyage was the expedition so solemnly organised to ancient Egypt. It commenced with the young man at the far table who persistently swaggered about his travel adventures, and made himself so easy a prey to the insurance broker, the planter and the Polish forester who sat at his table. As he talked of Japan as though he had discovered it, or related marvellous adventures in the East, these three spurred him on with questions of delicious naïveté, and listened open-eyed to his replies about Geisha girls and rickshaws. Thus flattered he talks louder and louder until the joke is taken up by neighbouring tables, and he is plied everywhere for further descriptions of his adventures.

Travelling Companions

"How splendid it must be to be so well off," sighs the planter, and the victim modestly denies the possession of vast wealth, but claims to be an "open-air plant".

"Open-air," they demand, "what's that? What do you say?"

"Yes, indeed. To be merely rich, to go to expensive schools for many years, what is the use of that in practical life? It breeds hot-house plants, sir. Life alone makes you a man. I may have had some good luck, of course. But mainly I think I can claim to be a self-made man."

"Doubtless you have been in Egypt too?" insinuates the broker. "That must be a wonderful country." He bows his head with the too-careful parting of the oiled hair, and there is a glint in his fox eyes which betokens trouble.

"No, I'm afraid not yet," admits the other. He can be modest enough when circumstances demand, but his immediate "Have you been there?" suggests that he will brook no trespassing on his territory of travel talk.

"Unfortunately not. But I hear we may get an opportunity. The Captain intends to have the screw inspected at Port Said. Do you remember that we had a slight shock in the North Sea when we collided with that whale? The water was dyed red with its blood you recollect. Since that the Captain believes he has noticed a certain irregularity in the rotation, and before taking the ocean he wants to have the thing examined. It may take one day, it may take two; and I have a plan. As soon as we arrive at Port Said we will go ashore and explore Ancient Egypt together. We make a detour, go on to Suez by train, and rejoin the boat there after it has made the day's journey down the canal. That will give us three days. Would any one else care to join us?" His beady eyes managed to convey things to the listeners which passed unnoticed to the young man in search of more travel tales. He nods again as he receives some assent. "Excellent, then we go to see the old, old Pyramids. Nothing could be simpler. The wireless man will send a message to Cooks and the camels will be waiting for us when we reach Port Said. All we need do is to decide how many we need."

"And what it will cost," dryly suggests the Pole who has suddenly shown a practical turn of mind.

By this time their victim is agog with excitement for the expedition. He is already in Egypt in his fecund imagination, and agrees that they must inquire as to the cost.

An Artist in the Tropics

"That also can be ascertained by wireless," replies the broker, realising now that his kite will fly, and soon he has a sheet of paper and is making a list of the proposed party.

"That's six camels, *und,*" he queries the Norwegian engineer in German, "*Für Sie und die gnädige Frau ein Doppeltkamel?*" The Norwegian being in a state of mild hysteria, other married couples stake their claims to a double camel, whilst the broker explains that it is fashionable for married couples to share a beast each sitting on one hump.

In the evening during dinner, by arrangement with the wireless man who is in the conspiracy, the wireless reply is brought in. The number One Chinese hands the form, which reads "Reduction of tariff just begun has caused great demand for camels. Two short can be replaced by giraffes. Wire reply. Cook."

The Pole proposes to the still innocent butt of the joke that they shall be the giraffe riders; but that gentleman begins to suspect the *bona fides* of this fantastic journey to Old Nile, and perhaps it was unnecessary to invent the Captain's decision that the screw would need no attention. A glance at that potentate's face behind his serviette settled the matter.

There are other minor plots, alarums and excursions during the voyage. Mr. Volski, for example, who brought a special gramophone on board to provide some new steps for some extra dances, and who until a certain period was a boisterous soul willing at the least provocation to sing arias from the operas in a shrill tenor voice, suddenly became morose. In his case it was the gramophone which caused the trouble, for he began to worry everybody with the scheme of joint purchase of it as a souvenir to the ship, and to say that the idea was received unenthusiastically is an understatement of the case. One gentleman, and that his table companion, went so far as to express his preparedness to purchase the whole affair if he might be allowed to throw it into the sea. Whereupon these two no longer share their regular bottle of wine.

Thus the little jokes and little acrimonies, superficial friendships and transient enmities fill the long and empty days. In the meantime Mrs. Brown has taken everybody into her dear confidence and unveiled a corner of her journeyings along life's path, until one discovers that every other single person on the boat seems also to be the lady's bosom confidant.

Travelling Companions

And when, at long last, the end of the journey is arrived, the Captain makes his final little speech, complimenting himself courteously upon his good luck in having so pleasant a company of passengers. Like Mrs. Brown's now famous confidences, it becomes impossible to guess how often that speech has been made before, or will yet be made. But we dare to believe it true.

Chapter Three

Port Said

AFTER the grey North Sea, the known European sights, we have gazed at the romantic coast of Africa, far and enticing, and woven about it our own dreams. Morocco, Tangier, the mauve and green hills of Algeria, every place the steamer passed conjured its own vision of white mosques, Bedouins in gleaming burnous, long-bearded Arabs, narrow passages, lively markets, lattice windows. These in our fancy, for of them we saw nothing but gliding shadows of clouds over the undulating land and white dots which were the teeming cities. So we passed. Then came the bare, treeless Malta, lightly colouring the scintillating blue surface of the sea. Still we passed. But at last—Port Said. The pilot has come on board, and through the mild summer evening air we glide quietly into the harbour. This is the very Orient, and to-morrow we shall tread its streets.

Suddenly the circumscribed life of our own shipboard is brought into vivid contact with the bustle of the great harbour: passenger steamers as crowded as our own; silent, tremendous men-of-war; little, lightly-dancing scallops; quays, houses, pilot-boats, lights. More and more slowly we feel our way to anchorage. Immediately the anchor is lowered the waters around us are interlaced with boats full of strange folk. The landing stairs are let down with much rattling of chains, and at once shouting and gesticulating Orientals crowd aboard. First come the officials and local authorities— police, postal and customs-house men, imposing fellows these, with red fez and fiercely bright yellow boots; they sport big medals on their chests and wear tremendous moustaches like oriental potentates in comic opera. Following this official influx comes an amazing assortment of strange riff-raff of the East in turbans

COAL RAFTS, PORT SAID (*Drawing*)

Port Said

and fluttering head dresses, long dowdy robes, dirty rags and every kind of tawdry garment, their keen faces every shade of brown. Some youths among our passengers, in ecstasy at this wealth of oriental sensation, cheer hysterically and shout "pshaw", "bo" and "Ali-Baba!" to the visitors.

Down below, on the water, the Babel increases. All types of traders, money-changers and divers swoop down on us. One of the divers makes himself heard above the din: "Say, Mister-r-r Macgregor-r! Thrrow shilling! I fetch. I dive!" and he gesticulates passionately, splashing the water with brown glistening limbs. Several shillings are thrown down; he "fetch" them with alacrity, but "dive" he does not, only demanding "One more, Misterr Macgregorr, I dive under ship." The promise increases his fee by several shillings, but still he does not "dive", and at last, when the inducement wanes, he swims calmly off to his boat and rows away to another ship there to invoke other generic Macgregorrs.

In the fading light we stroll on deck amidst the uproar; or watch, over the side, the great coal rafts as they slowly draw near the steamer, looming fantastically through the gloom.

The coal rafts are a bizarre dream. In the lights of flaming pots of fire, hanging and dangling at the ends of long iron rods, leap the shadows of Levantines, Arabs and varying negro types. As they come near, the hubbub and the clamour become deafening; everybody shouts the best way to bring the rafts alongside. Men in sack-cloth and filthy shirts, who at first were lying asleep on the coal, rise and join in the quarrel, or stretch their thin, brown hands towards the warming fires eagerly. Then suddenly the dazzling lights of our own boat shine out, and in their glare a giant leaps to and fro in frantic effort to catch the rope thrown to bring the rafts to us. With legs wide apart he stands on two floating logs which are to be the gangway. He pulls and lashes, and behind him the others come. They shout hoarsely with outlandish noises and stretch their arms dramatically in the air, or gesticulate towards one another with thin, bony hands.

One of them stirs frantically with a long stick in the fire so that flaming pieces of coal fly about to be trodden on without being heeded. Elsewhere a couple of baskets catch fire and a dozen fellows gather about them and shout and shriek and buzz there.

At last the rafts are roped alongside and work can begin. To the rhythm of a regularly repeated, long call the gangways are towed

An Artist in the Tropics

into position; the coal is shovelled into baskets and these are lifted high on the shoulders, two rows of human figures form themselves, one coming, one going; and unending, unvarying, inhuman, like the nervous pulsing of ants along an ant path, the work goes forward till far into the night.

The next morning a motor launch brings us ashore, and perplexed for a little, we find ourselves on the sunny quay of Port Said. There is something kinematographic about the feeling; the speedy launch puffing among the crowd of sleepy, rolling sampans; the disembarkation with an importance befitting a prime-minister beneath Pathé's eye; the first strolling through the sunny streets among the swarming Orientals; veiled Egyptian women, Arabs, mules, obtrusive brown pedlars who offer for sale every variety of thing, flowers, fruits, fans, ladies' bags, postcards, and most frequently their guidance without which they assure you you will be irremediably lost. The restaurants are gay with wide-spreading sunshades beneath which men play at cards or smoke Turkish nargilehs. Amidst it all, we pale Europeans, lightly-dressed tourists all, with parasols and white helmets: the fashionable ladies with high-heeled shoes, and gentlemen hung about with the inseparable Kodak.

The town itself seems a film come to life. Nothing is real; nothing is genuine. It is born of everything which is bad in the East allied to all that is bad in the West.—"Kermesse d'été" at a world's fair, a fancy dress ball in the open air, one big shop of rubbishy, quasi-oriental carpets, vulgar necklaces of coloured glass, cigarettes, bric-a-brac, brooches, souvenirs made in Germany and Brummagem.

The houses have wooden galleries in front with balconies at every floor. The footpath runs beneath these, but so numerous are the vendors who proffer their wares for sale to the tourists that one can hardly walk .

"Turkish delight? Nice, lady! Hollander? Lekker zeg? Here, Two shillings? No! One-and-six, here,. here! No? Two for one-and-six; look here, you feel. Quite full."

We are already growing wise to the Eastern salesmanship methods and decline firmly to buy a half-empty box of sweets.

If one sits down for a cup of coffee at the terrace of a restaurant, it is the signal for the arrival of half a dozen importunates with cigarettes, postcards or bracelets; in the meantime little boys are

Port Said

pulling at one's boots with their small monkey fingers to indicate their need of brushing. We laugh at a sly conjurer; some of us allow ourselves to be most speciously deceived by a fortune teller who strikes an imposing attitude for his task; a negro at a bookstall almost entices us to step inside by his obsequiousness. He has noticed that we lingered longer before the Dutch books in his window than before the others, and he grins encouragingly. He endeavours to get rid of a very old weekly paper at about seven times its original value, and when we indicate its date and nod in refusal, he pleads with us to come inside in broken Dutch which comes near to achieving its purpose.

A policeman, strangely sporting a fez and riding a beautiful Arab horse, passes along the glaring, sunlit street—an appealing mixture of comedy and beauty. The water-carrier also passes; a brown man of some incredible inter-mingling of races, he loiters with his shining brass cans and beats his ringing cymbals in the sunlight or chinks them alluringly. Before him he carries a large earthenware pitcher, a kind of amphora, with ice at the top to cool its contents. When a little client comes in a wide, white robe, our water vendor first rinses a glass which he carries at his belt with some water from a tankard, then bending forward he dispenses his cool beverage from the exquisitely polished spout of his jar.

Rembrandtesque beggars shuffle along the streets, or sit like Biblical figures under the porches, dozing or muttering. Insolent, rapacious women pass, dressed in black and veiled to the eyes.

Unexpectedly we arrive at a Square, with a shrubbery and fencing in European style. Drawn by the invitation of green shade or some nostalgia to the trees and bushes we are thrilled to find borders of nasturtiums, blue monkshood and scarlet salvia. The ugly bust of De Lesseps which stands in the centre cannot spoil our enjoyment; we turn to the somewhat neglected borders full of summer flowers blooming in these early April days under the Southern skies.

So we return with a coloured memory of our day, of the strayed glory of homeland blossoms amid the multi-coloured Eastern life and tawdriness, the dirt and untidiness, the World's Fair atmosphere of the town.

Kinema-like still, the self-important puffing little launch brings us back to our steamer, and Port Said becomes a reminiscence as we sail onward to the real East.

Chapter Four

A Cyclone

"WELL, Captain, what of the weather?"

We were well out in the Indian Ocean. The rolling of the ship, the intense, increasing heat, the oppressive air, made the question more than usually relevant. Moreover, this evening was dedicated to the concert which was to be our contribution to the community. Card-playing, deck tennis, the Chinese Gamble, or the more vigorous amusement of tug-o'-war, had wilted under the menace of the heat, and we wondered if the weather would upset our plans whilst the passengers were anticipating the music which was to beguile their evening.

Everything had been prepared. The piano had been unscrewed and put at the other side of the saloon, the engineer had provided footlights, for which the carpenter had made a wooden box, and two powerful electric lights mounted in big tins made limes worthy of the appearance of a prima donna. Two tables had been unscrewed and taken away to make room for our stage and auditorium.

The Chinese boys and servants stared amazedly at these preparations, grinning kindly. "Film, film?" one asked with a wink implying deep knowledge of European activities. We denied the allegation, but our explanations of the facts failed lamentably to explain.

By the time everything was ready and our concert began the wind had risen to something like a gale; everything was being blown about the place and our limelights added quite superfluous heat as well as their wonted candle power. All the flies which were *en voyage* with us attended the concert; they harassed the accompanist, resting appreciatively on his hands, his ears, his eyes, his neck, and on his music.

THE RED SEA *(Drawing)*

A Cyclone

Every now and again the Captain went to the bridge: at first he essayed to keep the vessel quiet by adroit steering, later he abandoned hope of quietude, and sought to bring her back to the original course. With the increase of the storm the difficulties of musical production increased also, and by the time the performance was brought to an end the elements were in full career. Everything that was not fixed flew to and fro through the cabins. From each of them came thuds and shrieks, and in our own a spate of books from the wardrobe preluded the tremendous smash of the electric fan to the floor.

Then lightning blazed across all other sights, and thunder drowned all other sounds, in a violence which only the tropics know.

Outside the portholes the lifeboats were silhouetted at one moment against the blazing West, at the next they were gleaming in the ghostly blue pallor of the flashes to the East. From the decks came the sound of hasty running, calling and shouting, for the swimming tank which the Captain had had constructed from heavy beams and planks with canvas, was blown to pieces. The Chinese crew, whose incomprehensible babble sounded ghoulish, laboured in the darkness overhead.

Harder lashed the torrential rains and wilder the waves beat over the ship. Something crashed at the onslaught of a head sea, and with a tremendous smashing of timber the gangway which had been torn off was flung up three decks and dashed to pieces on the Captain's deck.

Then the storm centre drew away from our battered ship, but even so it was impossible to lie still. After a few hours daybreak came, a dawn unreal and horrible waking in the livid skies. Waves like toppling hills; prehistoric monsters, leaden-grey, curving their backs as they bore down upon us one behind the other. We could see into their serried ranks, three or four deep; then sight ended in the grey mist which hung over the seas, the hot spume of moisture which hemmed in the ship. The stern plunged into the shelving waters as though we were ploughing straight to the bottom, the waves breaking heavily still across her deck.

One after another, pale and sleepy, the passengers came upstairs, clinging bunglingly for support to anything which offered. Many of them did not appear. All through the day the dull grey light

An Artist in the Tropics

remained. Hour after hour the mist, the head seas, the rolling of the ship, continued, and it was late in the afternoon when the murk became a little lighter, a little less livid and sinister.

Somebody diagnosed our experience as a little bit of a cyclone which went off in the direction of the Gulf of Bengal. We asked the Captain whether he had known that. He lowered a lid with a seaman's wisdom.

"We are like the doctors," he said, "we find it best to tell our patients what has happened after the event."

Chapter Five

Penang

SKY, water; water, sky.

Sixteen days of monotonous voyaging have made the ship a prison. Every day seemed endless. How soon one feels isolated on the sea, cut off from the world, longing for contact again with the familiar earth.

At limitless seas, at ever-empty skies we have been gazing, surrounded by an eternal monotony. The Indian Ocean had failed us. Had we not dreamed of finding fairy tales of iris colouring and fabulous beauty? Surely we were to peer into water grotto's of deep blue and venomous green, wherein would be fantastic swarming of strange fish, gorgeously coloured. The sky would be of mother-of-pearl brilliance by day, and by night virgin blue embroidered with the twinkling, golden stars.

So we had pre-ordained it; but alas, for the reality. Those marvellous sea-gardens must be somewhere away in the far Molucca Islands, and the fantastic dreams broke and dissipated against the dull realities of an ordinary grey sea and an ordinary grey sky, day after day, day after day. The only thing to be seen in the enormous stretch of the seas would be a prosaic steamer in the distance, very like the one we were on ourselves, signalling politely that all was well on board. Starved as we were for sensation, we would crowd to the side of our ship to look at that flutter of flags or, if it were evening, the tiny, twinkling lights. After that—again nothing. The first school of flying fish skimming over the water thrilled us for a moment or two; soon we grew blasé, and nobody took interest in them any more. The cyclone alone had broken the spell; then the eventless regularity closed down upon us again, the penetrating screech of the ship gramophone and the senseless wobbling of dancing passengers emphasising rather than alleviating it.

An Artist in the Tropics

And then Penang.

Truth to tell it does not look inviting from a distance. The sky is hard and blue, as though it were of painted steel; against it the palms glimmer cruelly green; white and pink buildings stand like large iced cakes along the painted shelf of the yellow quay—the whole view has the crudity of the cheap coloured postcard, the inartistic, utilitarian postcard which one purchases *faute de mieux* to announce an arrival. We would forgive Penang any appearance, however, for the fact that at last we may go ashore.

The real East we are to see at last; we shall be able to walk about, we. . . . But immediately the cohorts of the wise are upon us. "Walk about!" they exclaim, "Impossible, quite impossible. To begin with it is far too hot in the middle of the day, and moreover, no European goes on foot in the tropics; you take a rickshaw." A little daunting this, and we consider whether we shall wait as we are advised until after four o'clock before essaying the shore. But the pink and white houses and the sharp-leaved palms across the blinding glitter of the water are too tantalizing, and with a few other impatient passengers we take boat to the quay.

At moments it seems that the wiseacres are right. The skin of one's hands and neck is burned red in a few minutes, the asphalt is soft and slippery and sticks to the soles of our shoes, we lower our lids against the dazzling whiteness of the sunlight and quickly take refuge in the narrow strip of shadow against the houses. Everywhere the Chinese with their rickshaws crowd our way. They are desperately persistent; they stand full in our way, they walk along with us, they cross our path; they cry ceaselessly with hard thin voices "Ho, ho, rickshaw." We shake our heads as persistently, knowing that no luxury of rickshaw riding could compensate for the joy of feeling the solid earth beneath our feet. But the rickshaw men know nothing of these subtleties; they know only the tradition that a European does not walk, and it is long indeed before they realise that we are the sort of Europeans who do the things called "impossible" by our more traditionally-minded fellows. As their persistence flags, their chances of success increase if only they knew. For the heat is stifling. No longer may we be said to walk; we lounge. Slowly, still more slowly we dawdle. Yet we do not regret the excursion.

In Penang for the first time we see the Chinese in their own streets and houses. The charm which emanates from a Chinese

CHINESE HOUSES (Drawing)

Penang

quarter, with its picturesque houses, shops, temples and fine out-lines of gables, has taken possession of us; afterwards in many a new town it will prove to be almost the only thing of architectural value. Now we think no longer of picture-postcards; here we stand face to face with the life of the East itself. Every building is open in front; both houses and shops have a wide porch, and we see the industrious Chinese busy with their multitudinous craft. Some, squatting on their hassocks in the doorway, are eating out of rice bowls; others praise the quality of the goods they offer for sale, the matting and hurdlework, the silks and woven material, all kinds of pastries, dried fish and fruits.

Here is the barber shaving his clients. Yonder, in the street also, sits the dentist with his patient in front of him seated on his hassocks, his mouth wide open as in agony whilst long hooks and pins are skilfully manipulated among his teeth: a Jan Steen picture translated into Chinese. Children with keen, mouse-like eyes bristle around us. Colour is everywhere; on clothing and imple-ments, painted doors, gilt letters, enormous paper lanterns, on the strange confectionery and stranger fruits.

After a while we pass through broad avenues to the shadowed terrace of a hotel at the sea-shore. Under enormous trees we rest, and take respite from the crowded sensations of this new life under tropic skies. Even here the giant trees and vegetation force our interest. All our lives we have known them as pictures in books and prints, but they hardly became real to us; here before our eyes they are little more convincing, so unfamiliar are their shapes and hues. A fan tree spreads its fine shape, unbelievably two-dimen-sional, flat against the hard blue behind; near by, coconut palms seem comparatively commonplace against the gigantic trees beyond. Some have wide tops covered with orange-red flowers shaped like lilies; others have hanging bunches, vaguely resembling our laburnum in form, and glorious in white, yellow and lilac blossom. The air is heavy with the drowsy scent of the camellias. All about us, in a perfect blaze of colour, rise the wonderful convoluted trunks; high over our heads the long air roots feed the giant vegetation. In these luxurious gardens the airy, lofty houses of the wealthy Chinese stand.

Late in the afternoon the Chinese ladies stir abroad. In little groups of six or eight they sit in their automobiles like stone idols, looking straight before them, motionless, static as they take their

An Artist in the Tropics

little drive. Richly embroidered jackets they wear; their faces, powdered white as chalk, seem calyxes of exotic flowers, and in their night-black hair which is pulled back straight, they have small pink bouquets, white garlands or gold pins. With their waxen, immobile faces they look like porcelain dolls.

When dusk falls, and we are tempted to walk again in the cooler evening air, it is the Chinese quarter of the town which draws us instinctively. We hear a noise of brass gongs and big drums; shining lights radiate in the distance. In true Eastern fashion they are holding a stage performance in the open air. Gently we press through the hundreds of spectators, and soon we are as absorbed as they in the mysterious fable enacted by the great mandarin and the devilish scoundrel, the lady in her exquisite blue silk with her penetrating voice pitched much too high for Occidental taste, and the swiftly moving minor actors. As orchestral accompaniment, two little boys, almost naked, sit aside, and intermittently warble on their native flutes and snatch a mouthful of rice from wide bowls with their eating sticks.

The next morning we had planned an automobile journey to the temple of Ayer Itam, our companions an English cleric and his wife with whom we were sharing the cost of the car. The drive gave us our glimpse of rural tropic life as yesterday had shown us the town. Through palm woods, past bronze-brown Tamils lightly treading at the side of heavily-laden ox waggons, we drove to the village of rough wooden houses roofed with dry palm leaves, and alive with a noisy assortment of pigs, poultry and naked children. Beyond this a valley with a little brook running over blocks of stone, and then a steep mountain slope thickly overgrown with tropical vegetation. Behind it lay the Temple of Ayer Itam, the Black Water, a mass of buildings and terraces climbing the hillside and closed in on either side by hills crowned with cocoa trees. As we neared the Temple the road climbed more steeply, to the gate itself marked by two giant trees. On the steps as we came up sat the typical beggars of the Orient, dirty, covered in the most miserable rags, humming incomprehensibly or praying.

The great gate gave on to a courtyard across which we reached the big hall with a wide niche in the large wall containing hundreds of quaint Buddha images. Thence one goes to the higher terraces

Penang

inspecting on one the holy tortoises in a pond, and on yet another the goldfish in their basin. Everywhere there is a blaze of sunlight from a sky cloudless and seeming to be stretched taut by the heat. A few palms tower into the air, and terrace after terrace rises behind them, with steep stairs leading to more buildings. There are also, as the beggars who are acting as our guides most carefully point out, two shrubs shaped as English soldiers with glossy stone heads perched upon them—a topiarian homage to the English rulers of the country. This mixture of good and bad taste in the East ceases at last to shock. On one occasion when we were visiting a wealthy Chinese gentleman we were first impressed with the exquisite paintings, and the beautifully designed manuscripts, the poetic and calligraphic value of which were the just pride of their English speaking owner; but our politeness was strained to breaking point when we were called upon to admire equally a selection of the most vulgar paraffin lamps of the vilest European patterns and a glass bauble of more than two yards diameter as *pièce de milieu* at the ceiling.

After the shrub-soldiers our unsolicited guides direct us to the right where they explain, not without difficulty, is the accepted point for taking a snapshot. Our clerical friend hesitates for a moment, but his wife who makes the fourth of our party has every intention of doing the right thing.

"Everyone takes it from here," she says, and that settles the matter. The camera clicks and the honour of the party is saved. Higher again, and you arrive at the hall in which you are allowed to add your name to the Book of Distinguished Visitors. Plain, prosaic people from the West cheerfully face this duty of giving a small sum for the maintenance of the Temple and its priests (for the privilege of being a distinguished visitor has its financial drawbacks) but our friend the cleric finds himself on the horns of a dilemma. Shall he break the custom or support idolatry? His wife, ever decisive, says he cannot thus countenance the heathen, but he still feels that he should pay for the rare sight, and since all situations are soluble by compromise we each give our *obole*, but the secular members of the expedition alone admit it, and put down their names for both amounts. Thus we discharge our companion's mind of its conscientious objections by a little administrative irregularity which lies quite quietly on our own souls.

An Artist in the Tropics

The Hall of the Distinguished Visitors has its own treasures. A holy snake is there in a cage; many urns, vases, images in incredible numbers, some with kindly apple-cheeked faces, others grim and angry devils gesticulating passionately; with these are lots of paper flowers and many genuine ones, dishes with food, offerings, slowly-burning incense, hanging flags inscribed with Eastern lettering—anything and everything amazingly mixed for purposes and meanings we cannot guess but making an exotic picture to the painter's eye. Little as we can understand the symbolism of what we see or penetrate to the living forces which have builded this temple, somehow there emerges that intuition of an art and a religion having more potency than we casual visitors from the West can grasp. As we return down the great terraces, looking back every few steps at this exquisite harmony of architecture and nature, we get a glimpse of the secret of the East. The Oriental knows how to live in harmony with his universe, how to build without sacrilege amid the wonders of nature, how to walk, how to stand, to move, to be still. Moved beyond our Western reticence we turn to our companions.

"What do you think of all this?" we ask.

"Oh, awfully interesting, but very strange and bizarre, don't you think?" replies our clerical friend, and his wife adds her own comment about "all those gruesome images".

The tinkling little afternoon tea adjectives urge us to further effort.

"But the arrangement of the Temple, its situation, its building?"

"Oh yes! Very nice, very nice, it's quite true."

With mechanical certitude our automobile carries us back to the more familiar world.

Chapter Six

Travelling in the Land of the "Kompenie"[1]

"THINK of it!" (This, of course, is printed in capitals.)

THINK OF IT!!!

A man dishonours your sister, whom you love above everything in the world, and abandons her, dying, throwing her like refuse upon the streets; your dear mother dies of grief at her daughter's fate; your beloved fiancée is raped by this same villain, who, furious at her noble resistance, kidnaps her and takes her to a remote island of the Pacific, and out of bestial revenge sells her to the scum of Society, the hyenas in human form, who have sought refuge there;

AND THEN

This man, for whose blood you are thirsting, unexpectedly stands before you heaping insult and infamy on the woman you adore.

WHAT WOULD YOU DO?

What would one do? The hypothetical query reaches us as a Kinema advertisement as we sit, submissively, on the hotel verandah, in the interminable hours of the afternoon which stretch between the mid-day rest and the welcome beating of the dinner gong. If it moves us to any reaction at all it is to a faint desire to be appointed Governor-General and, in the interests of public decency, to forbid the thing being shown. One is more attracted to the varied fare announced

[1] The seventeenth century East Indian Company no longer survives, but its name, corrupted to " Kompenie," still remains as an idiom for the Government.

An Artist in the Tropics

by another circular which some unknown hand has placed upon the
hotel table. This is of the evening performance at the Club proffered
by the half-caste amateurs. It promises:

The Eurasian, before and after 1890 .	Pantomime
In the Groves of the Hague . .	Prologue
Hula Medley	Mandoline
Oh, this Sweet...!	Comedy Athletics
The Dirty Dog	Cabaret
Waikiki Mermaid	Hawaian Orchestra
The Step School	Song and Dance
Pua Carnation	Hawaian Trio
The Last Tooth	Cabaret
Henry's Puppets	Pantomime

INTERVAL

A Comedy in One Act:

"The Order is, 'Snore!'"

Sitting there in the heat we speculate dimly upon this Gilbertian
country where prologues succeed pantomimes. Nothing happens.
Sometime before dinner we shall have a drink, some time a bath.
Very occasionally a Chinese pedlar with silk and cotton goods will
disturb our peace; the crowds of beggars, newsboys, chocolate-sellers,
and touts for backstreet cafés who besiege one at the railway stations
have been left behind in Europe. Indeed there is no country where
one can travel so quietly and easily as in the East Indies. One is
never stranded. Coolies are always available to carry the luggage,
and with them the tiny go-carts upon which to load it. What quantities
they take! Travellers, trunks, bags, rugs, wraps and all kinds of
gear and always the driver himself manages to find a perch, even
though it be a perilous foothold crouching on the off-side, or swaying amazingly on top of the pile. At times, however, as for example
when we came to Solo, there is a "kareta" from the hotel, and then
one arrives in royal style, the ceaseless cracking of the whip heralding
a magnificent approach.

In the Land of the "Kompenie"

At the hotels luggage is as safe as in any good European hotel. Our unlocked bags remain untouched, despite the stories we have been told of luggage stolen or rifled, lost or "gone before". Having travelled in Java for many months, carrying always a considerable amount of luggage, and never having lost anything even though we left our trunks open, we feel safe in assuming a deal of exaggeration in these "traveller's tales", and pay our tribute to East Indian honesty.

The hotels in the big towns are excellent as a rule. Off the beaten track and in the smaller places there are certain things to which a European does not easily become accustomed. *L'eau courant* and lavatory basins fitted, in up-to-date manner, in the bedrooms, with a waste pipe down to the bathroom sink will happen in places such as Macassar; but away from these it is still customary to empty the washing basins straight out of the rooms into the yard, plop, plop, plop, one after the other, just as it was described by Bas Veth in his cynical book upon Java written several decades since.

When guests arrive at a hotel and no proprietor or manager appears the only thing to do is to shout and wait till a "Mandoor", the native headwaiter, or a boy presents himself, as no house, hotel or other building has a bell or a knocker. The non-appearance of the manager may be taken as a bad portent; it invariably means that the house is kept by somebody who regards his destiny as being above that of hotel management, and who continues throughout your stay to indicate this. It is thus brought home to the traveller that it is a great favour to be allowed to stay on the premises, until he flies, pursued by nightmare memories of this condescension intermixed with those of the cocoanut oil which made every meal loathsome, and of the vast but inscrutable bill which acted as epilogue to the adventure.

Respect for the great ones of the earth can be learned even in a hotel, or at least in the hotel at Mooara Enim, where since the visit of the former Governor-General more than five years before, his mosquito curtain had remained reverently untouched. The matter interested us the more as we were duly honoured by being put into the room thus immortalised; whereupon we dared to express the hope that it would show no lack of deference to the transient Governor-General if the mosquito-curtain were washed.

The inventory of a hotel room is generally quite simple: all costly etceteras have been eliminated. One bed, one chair, one

An Artist in the Tropics

washing basin, one table, one coat-hanger and a little oil-lamp completes the list, save in the expensive houses where some concession is made to comfort. Apart from these the furniture is reminiscent of the poorest second-hand auction rooms—rickety, worn-out and filthy. In towns which, like Medan, are considered large for the East Indies, it is not impossible to find the water for cleaning your teeth reposing on your wash-stand in a gin bottle; or at lunch the boy will pour the drinking water from one of those dark green bottles which gurgles so pleasantly with the well-known mark "Bokma, Leeuwarden". Even in one of the three big hotels at Sourabaya the teacups are kept in the passage behind the guest rooms in packing cases marked "Bols very Old Gin".

At first this may seem a little strange, but the traveller in the East will soon accustom himself to this mania for adapting things. One may get one's tea on a meat dish instead of a tray, the early morning coffee may have to be poured from a maggi-meat-extract bottle, the milk is in a damaged teapot. There are moments when this enthusiasm for economy seems to be overdone; moments when it becomes half-humorous in its ingenuity as when, for example, the borders of the paths are marked by long rows of inverted beer bottles with their heads buried ostrich-fashion in the sand. Too often, alas, they proved to be the only visible division between the path and the borders they were assumed to protect, so little division of kind was there between them.

One phenomenon of the hotels is the garden pots. Each hotel has a wide open space in front with a semi-circular drive for incoming and outgoing carriages sweeping up to the main block of building where the chief public rooms are. The rest of the guest rooms are built in two wings left and right of this main building with the kitchens, bathrooms and garages at the back. A garden does not exist. The front of the hotel ground is usually left just as it was before the hotel came, or is adorned with some rough gravel upon which the unwary walk as though they were dancing on eggs. Where garden should be, burgeon only the ubiquitous garden pots. In serried ranks and single files, in square formation or in geometric or amorphous figures, the heavy, earthenware pots are put down. Continuously bespattered with mould thrown up by the heavy rains, overgrown with moss, they form the eternal battle-ground of a struggle between the lime brushed on them for protection and

RICEFIELDS WITH BUFFALO (*Drypoint*)

In the Land of the "Kompenie"

the forces of nature. Flowers they seldom contain whatever may have been the original intention; but everywhere is green vegetation—palms and ferns, ferns and palms waving above this cemetery of pots.

The first time you become acquainted with this phenomenon you might surmise that the hotel proprietor is a retired potter who has adorned the premises in despair from the remnants of his former business. Once, at Madioon, we conceived the unholy notion of counting them, but when at four hundred and twenty we realised that we had but touched the fringe of this task our determination wavered and we vowed never to attempt the impossible again.

At many railway stations in Java one notices a native with a gigantic whip. He proves to be neither circus-master nor drover, but when, with a tremendous swing of his arm, he makes his whip crack louder than any hubbub which may be toward, he is revealed as a railway official giving the alarm that a train is coming in and that no one must cross the lines to the other platforms in the usual Javanese fashion. At the time for departure of a train a huge bell sounds twice as the signal that seats should be taken. After a minute the bell is rung three times, and subsequently a whistle is blown. Then everybody shakes hands and bids the voyagers good-bye and when that is finished the train is permitted to depart.

On arrival at a station it is not unusual to find that six or eight coolies have taken possession of your luggage, and you have to utter the magic formula, "Taxi" in a large town, or the equally potent "Sado" in a small one, or they will have vanished and loaded your belongings on a number of the small vehicles which exist in the East Indies in astonishing variety. An "ebro", a "sado", a "deelemannetje", an "andong", a "bendie", a "dokar", a "kossong" and whatever other names they may possess, each have a wheel more or a horse less than each other. The "Sado" is very like an ancient instrument of torture. The seat, on which driver and passenger sit *dos-à-dos*, is kept balanced over the one axle of the two-wheeled carriage by the skill of the driver himself. This, at least, is the theory of the thing; but on the rough cobbles of the roads the bascule occasionally dips, and as the seat slides to and fro and is sloping instead of horizontal, and the sado horse seldom deigns to pull straight but alternates to left and right, it is not so easy to stay in a sado as to conjure one with a word. Even when

33

An Artist in the Tropics

you have yourself become a virtuoso in sado-riding your trunks may find the task beyond their equipoise, and many a sado journey is interrupted whilst an errant trunk is rescued from the road.

If a carriage has four wheels and two horses as the "andong" of Mid-Java, it may be depended upon to go twice as slowly in spite of these facilities. To live in the East is to learn these paradoxes. One other pitfall is the assumption that experience in Eastern travel will make you wise as to the nomenclature of these vehicles; but the moment you move to a new place your old wisdom will no longer avail. In Singapore and many other places, for example, a carriage drawn by a Chinese is called a "rickshaw"; but in Palembang it is called "betja"; whilst the "deelemannetje" has become a "kareta". Further North, in Medan, the "betja" is a carriage with a horse instead of a Chinese as motive power, and the "betja" we have grown to know has become a "hongkong", so that the process is endless. Even the driver has another name which has blown with the East wind from the Straits Settlements.

Most of the vehicles have a characteristic trait common also to the Malay house of being not nailed but tied together. If a nail is found anywhere its chief function seems to be the retention of a piece of your clothes, for the Malay races have supplanted all its other functions by the knot. They even tie a number of pieces of wood together as an anchor for their boats and cause it to sink by adding a stone to the bundle. A great many of the carriages also have an appearance of having been frequently driven in and out of the water as a variation on their land activities. The "kossong" of Sourabaya is remarkable for the fact that the driver's feet are plunged into a tub of grass taken for a meal for a Rosinante compared to whom Don Quixote's steed must have been an Arab thoroughbred.

One other problem which confronts the traveller is that of finding your way in a Javanese town. As a rule the cab-driver knows nothing, but as it is impolite to say "No", the answer to any query as to such knowledge is an invariable "Yes", with a distressing disregard of the facts. Anyway his business instinct will forbid that he should risk losing a fare by a negation which has the further disadvantage of this lack of etiquette. Therefore he drives on—and on—and on, and when the unfortunate victim of this Odyssey has lost all idea of direction he will be carelessly asked

In the Land of the "Kompenie"

over the driver's shoulder whether he now desires that the carriage should turn to the left or the right. The hours lost in meandering "sados", however, are recovered in a flash when your native driver gets at the wheel of an automobile. To the European mind the native chauffeur and the native escaping a rainstorm are the only sudden things in all the leisured East.

Trains are driven in the day-time only, as the native engine drivers cannot be trusted to depend upon light signals; but in view of the difficulties with which the railways have to cope, the service, like that of the post, is admirable.

We must not omit to mention the almost sacred ritual of the rice-table, the mid-day tiffin. In Java it is as strictly *à-la-mode*, as in Sumatra it is not. The rice table at the hotels in small towns may not have the girth of the Tower of Babel but at least vies with that edifice for confusion of minds and tongues. Dietetic and other theorists will assert that rice is the food obviously intended by nature for consumption out in the East since it is the food grown in the country itself, and we were led to wonder often whilst the tiffin "dragged its slow length along" by what process of reasoning Dutch gin had taken so undisputed a place beside the natural product of the Javanese fields.

When tiffin is over, Oriental custom and the mid-day heat demand a siesta, and after that pyjamas and a rocking chair. This afternoon relaxation appears to be a source of some irritation to our globe-trotting American friends, who had never expected to discover such *sans-gêne* in the stolid Dutch, their ancestors. Java, they said, was the most wonderful country, but beyond any phenomenon of nature was to be accounted the pyjama displays on the hotel verandahs during the greater part of the day. We were glad for the honour of Java that no touring American was present in one town where the hotel guests were divided into a "dressed table" and a "pyjama table"; particularly as the hotel manager himself graced the "pyjama table" and therefore the choicest viands gravitated thither, and in their train ambassadors from the "dressed table" arrived with emphatic demands for a more reasonable distribution of food.

Despite these happenings so exotic to the European mind it is difficult at first for the traveller to realise that he is in the East. The houses are half-Dutch in the style of old country houses, with

An Artist in the Tropics

imitation-renaissance columns whitewashed respectably, but they all have the Malay open front verandahs. Neither the Dutch tiles nor the corrugated iron roofs which abound make a specifically Oriental impression, and it is only the ubiquitous palm trees and the stifling heat that impress the East upon us.

In some of the buildings are shops where trade goes forward with a casualness which again must disturb the thought processes of the exploring American. It is not unusual, for example, to be informed that some merchandise is sold out although quantities of it are visible. This fact demonstrated, the shop girl will giggle delightedly, straighten her hair at the mirror, and if her mood still holds good, deign to serve her customer.

Most towns have canals in imitation of the Dutch canals save that they have stone steps down to the water at either side to accommodate the natives, as they use the brown muddy water for many purposes. It is washing bath and swimming bath, latrine and tooth glass, children's playground and head-cleansing station; and is used alike by hotel boys, street vendors, and the staff from the Palace of the Governor-General. A little further down the laundryman is busy. He washes your white suits and underclothing, soaps it, rinses it and then beats it with much swinging of arms on a special plank, causing fountains of lather and making the legs of the trousers swing like the sails of a windmill.

Traffic between the islands is in the hands of the Royal Packet Navigation Company whose fleet of ships links up the whole archipelago. Mainly they are cargo boats, but they will also take a limited number of passengers. The accommodation and arrangements are quite good; sometimes simple, and sometimes luxurious as in the Australian liners with their cosmopolitan atmosphere. The other lines, however, are of a more old-fashioned type, homely and familiar if a little Spartan. First class passengers have dinner on deck with the Captain and the officers, which makes for interesting conversation if the passengers can set those nautical tongues wagging. Much depends, of course, in these circumstances upon the personality of the Captain; but generally these expert seamen are of the type who like to chat, and who have brought to these far seas some of the good, old-fashioned homeliness of Holland.

Thus it may happen that after dinner one may meet the old Dutch custom of well-wishing as the Captain murmurs softly behind

OLD HOUSES, BATAVIA (Drawing)

In the Land of the "Kompenie"

his serviette to his neighbour a "Much good may it do you", and then according to the immemorial rite everybody takes up the greeting muttering with a gentle nodding of the head "Muchgdmaytdyo," "Muchgdmaytdyo," "Muchgdmaytdyo".

In common with every big organisation, the Packet Company is the butt of much dissatisfaction. The general verdict is that it is extremely expensive, to which it is asserted that it is the monopoly which is at the root of all the Company's evil-doings. But the Dutch, never to be trifled with at home are even more violent in their protestations abroad. An army phrase has it that the Dutchman who does not "grouse" is ill, and as Dutch folk who were not ill we did our share of "grousing" at the Packet Company's vagaries, when, for example, the officials in the office did not know the best way to make a circular tour of a number of out-of-the-way places in the shortest possible time, or showed a blissful ignorance of time and place with regard to one of the boats we were destined to travel in. But the Board of Directors and the Powers-that-be at Headquarters assist everybody with a kindness which covers a multitude of minor incompetences; and these little inconveniences and difficulties alike are forgotten when one is on board, with the debris of a pleasant dinner before one, a Southern sky overhead, and the Captain and officers muttering their old world "muchgdmaytdyo," "muchgdmaytdyo."

Chapter Seven

Mount Salak in the Rain

BROAD is the land of the rice fields, flat as the meadows of Holland, stretching to where a volcano rises out of the endless plains. On every side the bright greens of the young rice plants in the "bibit" beds alternate with the dry yellow of the newly-cut ripe rice "padi", and the recently planted stems with their young green are delicately reflected in the pale blue of the water. In this great open plain is no fragrant growth, no wealth of happy field flowers, of full, rich foliage, nor the luxury of undergrowth which the Northerner would imagine there. Nor does the tropic East know the vital rhythmic change of the seasons. The sun, a fierce glare of blinding light, dominates the silent land, day after day beating mercilessly from verge to verge of the horizon. Rainless and exposed the low lands lie defenceless beneath its rays.

In regions such as the Preanger Regencies, or the East part of Java, the volcanoes have broken the ground, and piled it in hummocks so that the landscape has the appearance of some herd of creatures, close pressed, back to bowed back, or like some undulating ocean coagulate in storm. In that tremendous landscape man stands as a pigmy.

So from day to day, from week to week, unvarying in the sun-glare, burns orient Java. Then high above the wide plains volcanic Salak draws to its head the clouds, higher and higher like a garland about it, till suddenly the thunder rumbles, and in a wild, tumbling cloud, darkness rolls down the slopes. Swiftly the heavy cloudbank draws across the flat lands, the last gleams of light vanish from the smooth palm crowns crackingly swinging in the racing wind. The rain pours down in unsubdued torrents, bringing down with deafening din the broad leaves. It is a scourge, a plague of Biblical grandeur. The

Mount Salak in the Rain (*Drawing*)

Mount Salak in the Rain

water gushes down the hills, makes runnels between the slopes; roads become brooks; then muttering and foaming, it pours away into the Kali.

The natives have all fled suddenly. When the first drops fall the men cover their heads with their jackets, the women envelop themselves hastily in the carrying-scarf, the slendang, which hangs from their shoulders. As no native peasant ever goes about without a hatchet, some cut off a leaf from a banana tree, which with its thick stem like a stick and the broad fringe of the leaf, hardened, glossy as a tarpaulin, forms a natural raincoat, enabling them to walk on quietly.

After a time, the deluge may stop just as suddenly as it had begun. Immediately it seems that all the superfluous water has been swallowed by the soil. Still some drops gleam on the trees in the first rays of the sun as it breaks through the clouds, but they quickly evaporate, and the lacquer-green vegetation shines brighter than ever in the blinding arrows of the sun.

The village life takes its normal course again. Coolies come with their burden carried across their shoulders on swinging bamboo sticks; women, with their merchandise piled high in baskets on their heads—majestic figures, erect as statues—pass by with their swinging gait. Mothers carry their babies to the brook and bathe them with care; other women bring their laundry and in the Soondanese [1] manner they soap it abundantly until the water is afoam with lather. Bathers, male and female, move freely among them, unembarrassed in their natural chastity. The village girls leave behind their outer garments on a stone or thrown over a branch, pull up the sarong—which usually falls like a skirt from the waist—until it is beneath their armpits, and stride like princesses into the water—children of nature as they are. After the bath, the new dry length of the sarong is thrown loosely around the body, then with a dexterous movement of their flexible hands they tighten it at the back, bring the superfluous length in a simple fold in front of the body and twist the edge in at the waist to form its own belt. The discarded sarong, meantime, has slipped away beneath their new garment. The whole change takes but a minute, the simplicity, the ease, the unembarrassed

[1] The Soondanese live in West Java. Mid-Java is populated by the Javanese proper, in East Java a good many Madurese are found who settled there from Madura Island. Each are a race apart and have a language of their own.

An Artist in the Tropics

beauty of the action lingers long in the mind of the Western onlooker cramped with the conventions and inhibitions of civilised life.

To most Orientals the bare native body, beautifully shaped, has no erotic significance; the nude torso is as normal, as unprovocative, as the nude hands and face to the Western European. It has been pointed out that in the antique world this condition of nudity was natural so that the marbles of Praxiteles do not give us the feeling of the human body with the clothes stripped off which is inherent in a Rembrandt or a Titian nude, since by the time of the Renaissance custom demanded clothes. Lack of insight into this psychology of clothes has worked irreparable harm in the East, as the Western zealots have imposed upon the natural chastity of the natives their own cult of physical morality which merely results in imposing impure thinking.

The Indies are a different country not only with other trees and other folk but with other sentiments, other ideas than our own.

A Javanese, for example, does not easily say "No"; at least he does not say it to a superior, and therefore not to a white man, for to his mind the white man is the ruler. Students of the race may quarrel learnedly as to whether this custom is recent or has been acquired centuries since under the ancient Javanese rulers; but howsoever it came it is a factor to be reckoned with in one's relationship with the Javanese. To him it spells bad manners, impoliteness. Accordingly he will cheerfully say "yes" and act . . . "no". Politeness? Mendacity? Right you are if you think so!

How far this difficulty goes! We hardly recognise as a civilisation any other than our own. To the contemporary European, intoxication is a sign of lack of culture, a piece of bad behaviour. To drink with the preconceived idea of getting drunk would be rightly regarded as boorish. At the poles asunder lies the idea of philosophic discourse, the highest most abstract form of culture this, to discuss the essential values and meanings of life with a nobleness and sublimity which gives to the record of the conversation a sublimity through the centuries. Then we remember the instance when Plato, Socrates and their circle agreed that on a particular evening their customary intoxication might be suspended without discourtesy in view of the happenings of the previous day. Strange paradox this for our friends to whom temperance and culture are one, for who shall judge between Plato drunk and your modern teetotaler sober.

Mount Salak in the Rain

The native Javanese rarely gets drunk; his religion forbids. To him a drunken man is barbaric even though the man be white. Yet the white man is a builder of bridges, of railways, of automobiles. But which is the more civilised depends upon our conceptions of values. If one's viewpoint is "ethical", as they would say in the East, he over-estimates the refinement of feeling and the intuitions of the native and under-estimates the material and intellectual achievements of the West. Meantime the son of modern Europe swears by wireless and aeroplanes, and regards it as an advance to listen-in to nothing and fly to nowhere, losing beneath material excellence the ideal calm and poise of the East. The machine worship of the nineteenth century stands before our love for the things which are truly divine in our community; religion and the arts. It poisons by its very perfection, filling the world with imitation products which boast that they cannot be distinguished from the genuine.

This technical madness is at the farthest remove from the attitude to life of the Javanese native. He lives in much closer contact with nature, and his emotions vibrate in subtle harmony with it. To those of us who have become estranged from nature this rapport will be called eerie, gruesome, "black magic"; and by others more psychically-minded it may be termed super-natural and be regarded as a refinement of feeling. To the first it is matter for aversion, vexation; to the others appreciation and a kind of reverence. Truth probably lies somewhere between the two extremes.

The instinct for direction which causes a pigeon to fly homeward from some far, strange place, enables a native to speak of North or South, East or West even when he has about him no objective guide. Like his feelings his music is in close contact with nature. The native orchestra, the "gamelan", seems like nature's own sounds transported into the instruments: wistful and rustling like the wind over the ricefields, chirping like the birds in the bushes, pattering softly as the water flowing from one ricefield to another. Being based entirely upon the principle of rhythm it fills the time-space (marked by beats on a drum) with a liberty of melody unknown to Western music and therefore incomprehensible to us at first. Music, in common with the arts and crafts of the East Indies, has made but little appeal to those who have little understanding even of their own æsthetic products: but, on the other hand, these things

An Artist in the Tropics

have roused tremendous enthusiasm in some Western students who have found new values in them.

Interwoven with this intense feeling for nature which influences so much in Javanese life is the old Polynesian belief in ghosts, phantoms and gods. It still holds sway in the child-like minds of the natives, even though Hinduism has come and gone, and Islam has superseded the religion of old India.

Thus women still offer to an old Durga statue to invocate fecundity. Who this Durga was, they have long since forgotten. But to their naïve minds her sculptured presence has some strange power, and this must be favourably pre-disposed. The children of materialistic Europe may sneer at this "barbarity", with a calculated forgetfulness or ignorance of the strange origins of some of their own "Christian" feasts and festivals, and an equal disregard to their own proclivity to invoke influential powers.

So runs this eternal paradox of East and West. Near Batavia, in a place where old refuse iron is stored near an ancient gateway, lies a discarded cannon barrel. Long dismantled, it lies there in the grass, powerless to Western eyes but potent and holy to the Javanese. Women kneel and pray to it, holding it to have the power to fertilise; they offer flowers. Sagas have arisen round it. One of them predicts that one day a second cannon will be joined to this, and on that day the reign of the white man will cease in Java. Along the road past the sacred cannon whirls ever and anon the ubiquitous automobile, and natives pass barefoot. Car-worshipper, fetish-worshipper; by what standard of values shall we decide which is the richer? True the land is managed by those who do agriculture scientifically, who cultivate, grow, organise, construct roads and railways, and erect factories. Hurrying from one of their gods to the next go the ceaselessly active Europeans. Here and there, sacred, stepping aside as it were from this onrush of civilisation an old cannon which is deemed holy, a holy grave; and before it the Oriental lost in reverie.

High above everything, endless, immaculate, the volcanoes rise. They can be seen from miles and miles away across the flat landscape. Their solemnity and dignity demand solitude. They rest, imperturbably; or function, imperturbable still; hiding always latent forces whose might is unparalleled. Too vast for any human eye to encompass them, for the merciless fury of tropic sun the

" Canari-Trees, Botanical Gardens, Buitenzorg " *(Etching)*

Mount Salak in the Rain

deluges of tropic rains to harm them. Trees, villages, towns, railroads, factories, fetish-shrines, crouch at their feet; black man and white man; all things are transitory. Above all rise their torn bare cones. Centuries pass without leaving a trace. Nations, races, religions, come and go; there is no change. Only the volcanoes' eternal vigil.

Chapter Eight

A Holy Grave near Cheribon

To the average European no good thing can come out of, nor indeed
be near, Cheribon. "A wretched hole of a place" we were informed,
and in truth we found it to be only an old, almost forgotten, little
Javanese town with no attractions for the cosmopolitan visitor. No
jazz-music has yet made entry there, and in its quiet streets it is
only occasionally that the modernity of a motor engine disturbs
the peace. For those, therefore, who seek European counterparts
in the East, Cheribon, with its native simplicity, inevitably seems
a heaven-forsaken little place.

An old, open carriage, an old Javanese driver, an old horse
jogging along; thus we drive through its long shady avenues of
ancient trees with wide-flung branches protecting us from the heat.
Neither stateliness nor distinction can be claimed even for its wealth-
iest parts; the comparatively simple houses line the scarcely trodden
roads hidden by trees and shrubs, their back verandahs overlooking
tiny closed-in gardens. The eternally smooth sea lisps along its
beach by the town. In the poverty-stricken byeways, characteristic
and picturesque for all their squalor, Chinese traders earn precarious
livelihoods. It is undisturbed Java.

To be a guest in one of the quiet, better-class houses means
being really in the East—an experience after the business and royal
grandeur of one of the big hotels of Singapore or Batavia where
lively orchestras and unending gramophones bring the atmosphere
of the noisy European cafés into this primeval land. Our hostess
is occupied nearly all day at the experimental station for sugar where
she does some botanical work, leaving her guests to their own devices.
Sometimes, however, we go together and see the sun set at Wadook
Sedong or drive on the slopes of Mount Tjerimai. Even though

Entrance of a Temple, Cheribon *(Drawing)*

A Holy Grave near Cheribon

on one of these journeys we came near to forgetting that we were in Cheribon by being driven in a smart motor car, whose chauffeur, faultlessly dressed and sporting wonderful butter-yellow boots, was as up-to-date as our Javanese carriage Jehu was antique, we were brought to a sense of realities and given a lesson in Oriental resignation by the fact that he had brought out insufficient petrol so that the car came to a final rest in the darkness of the trees far from home. And there we were forced to leave it, guarded by the gentleman of the yellow boots whilst we walked home in the bright moonlight.

The main interest of Cheribon, however, lies on the hill beyond the outskirts of the town where is the grave of Sultan Goonoong Djati, the Founder of Mohammedanism in Java; and to this we made pilgrimage one day along the dusty roads beneath the tall, rough-barked, thin-leaved tamarind trees. Even before one reaches it a swarm of beggars and children come yelling towards one. In Java, it is true, beggars are seldom encountered, but here at the Holy Grave they abound, waiting in a swarm to leap upon their prey. The leap is literal statement of fact. Like cats they spring on to the car, clinging wherever they can obtain hold, and needing to be driven off before the hard-pressed occupants can alight. Wherever we go the whole pack of beggary goes with us. Shouting and pushing they swarm about us, a confusion of outstretched palms. One tries to arouse our pity, another stretches his arms stiffly in supplication, little boys whose sense of humour at their own insolence overcomes them, commence to mimic each other's whining and their own. We inquire of our hostess whether one gratuity would not exempt us from the unsavoury crowd, but she assures us that it would stimulate the rest to new activity, that they would stick to us like burrs at such a sign of generosity. When an opportune moment arrives, however, we throw a handful of coppers among the throng, leap into the car whilst they scramble for the booty, and drive off while the urchins are still rolling over the ground before they can invade our footboard again.

The hill is covered with graves, overgrown and dilapidated as they are everywhere: as are the Old Sumatra Sultans' graves; as the mouldy, time-worn, vaults of the ancient rulers in Madura Island, filled with fusty rubbish to honour their dead. The piled stones have fallen to pieces, roof-shaped mounds and upright head-

An Artist in the Tropics

stones alike are nearly perished with decay. High above the graves stretch the phantom trees with their bare, smooth trunks and their distorted branches raised as though to ward off evil. Beneath the trees a winding path leads up the hill. Miserable blind beggars, misshapen as fakirs, sit submissive in this actual place of tombs, waiting till Allah sends them a visitor who will award their patience—a deed pleasing to Allah. When we put a small silver coin into one of the skinny hands, the beggar fingers it again and again to ascertain its reality, and a strange smile lightens the dead face as he mutters unintelligibly a long prayer of thanks and blessing upon us.

On the other side of the road is the temple with the inaccessible grave of the Sultan. Again beggars, again children in importunate swarms ready to surround the hadjis who come to pray. Again blind men along the paths. The buildings climb the hillside stage by stage; now and again parts are surrounded by a wall, a whitewashed affair into which innumerable Chinese plates have been placed. Many of these have broken away subsequently, and sometimes the gap has been left, sometimes filled in with a vulgar factory-made European piece, with that astonishing mixture of taste and tastelessness which will astonish us many times more before the end of our tour. At every gateway the beggars sit. On the highest terrace accessible to infidels we find rows of Chinese vases blue and many-coloured, their bases fixed in mortar to the ground, their rims as high as our heads. Then again the graves continue.

A few hadjis on their hassocks mutter prayers in front of the ever-closed door behind which the grave of the holy Sultan lies. Some flowers are offered and money is given to the temple guards who pour consecrated water out of one of the immense Chinese pitchers. The believers whisper, then stillness falls about us, a silence real and palpable as the thick foliage which rises over the great Wall before us—the highest, the whitest, the last. Beyond it the grave lies, withdrawn from the world of sense and sight. Other hadjis come up gently, barefooted. Their wives accompany them with glittering gold-threaded coloured scarves on their heads, with painted eyes and fluttering gay garments. So eternally, unendingly the pilgrims come with prayers and gifts to the holy grave where Sultan Goonoong Djati lies asleep.

A Blind Beggar *(Drawing)*

Chapter Nine

In the Preanger Regencies, Java

BATAVIA and Bandoong are the two main towns of West Java; the first being the old seat of the Government, whilst the latter is striving to become the new one. Bandoong is situated much higher than its rival, therefore the nights are cool and the climate less stiflingly hot. The town is new and its houses are built after the style of our modern country houses and cottages.

South of the town a road leads past Tji Widei, bordered for some distance by ricefields of all shapes and sizes, lying flooded and glittering between their terraces; then, turning and wheeling round, the road plunges into wilder country, through deep ravines, always with the yawning precipices on the one hand and the shaggy heights above on the other. The flat, levelled, narrow strip of ground which forms the road, winds, twists and curls like a ribbon among the mountain landscape. A first motoring experience on its surface, with the car gasping, groaning and bumping over the stones in disconcerting proximity to the precipice edge whilst the grandeur of the Javanese mountains opens out continuously before you, is a strange mixture of the beautiful and the terrifying. Now and again the car seems to have breathing space on a piece of flat road, but only to plunge on into more hair-raising adventures wherein any slight mishap would mean the end of all things for the occupants.

But there comes an end to the too thrilling journey, and to the road through the mountains that seem to tumble around us. A white house at the foot of the virgin forests, a few more jolts and turns, a last steep slope, steeper it seems than any of its predecessors, and we stop before—a bed of flowers.

A bed of flowers! To the European motorist nothing could sound more natural and commonplace, but to us, weary and satiated

An Artist in the Tropics

by the everlasting, everspreading greenness, nothing could be more lovely than the sudden vision in these heights of a bed of roses—roses as we know them in the homeland, blossoming here in the mountains. There is a real house too, with glass doors and glass in the windows, and in the bedroom a bed with a blanket. The night is not merely a dark continuation of the day's heat; one no longer wrestles with the oppressive heat half in swoon, but settles down to refreshing sleep.

We look down upon a fresh, green meadow, dotted about with white and black cows, and with white houses like that in which we are going to stay. Spread out across the hilly landscape lie the woods of quinquina. Our host is Director of this government quinquina estate, and under the care of his guides we are taken to the interesting places of the locality.

One day a Soondanese will lead us through a maze of hills, where now and again a vast panorama would open out beneath us, or clouds would drift by hundreds of feet beneath our path. Narrower and narrower that path becomes; continually it is overgrown and with his hatchet he clears the way. Trees have fallen and lie sodden and rotting where they fell; long climbing plants hang like ropes from the trees; ferns of enormous dimensions, orchids with blade-shaped leaves grow on trunks and branches but their flowers are hardly noticeable in the shrill light. We climb over fallen trunks, we creep underneath them; all about us the vegetation hangs in a tangle. In a bush of thorny nettles a vanishing tail of a snake is the only sign of animal life. Startled by our coming, all living beasts lie hidden in their lurking places in this green, impenetrable mass.

As the forest thickens the light becomes more vague. A dead silence. The atmosphere grows more and more damp and close, the ground more sticky and slippery with half-rotten plants or stones and rocks covered with wet moss. If a tree stands, numerous parasites live on it: lianes bind it with their whirling sprays, and even these are overgrown with mosses and other tiny plants. Silently, they fight the life and death fight of nature, the struggle for survival. Hour succeeds hour as we pass through the impenetrable woods.

At last the murmur of mountain water is heard, and a moment after we see it glittering and splashing down from behind the rocks, the eternal, ungovernable force of the stream as it searches its way to the lower levels, there at last to slacken its energy and irrigate the

48

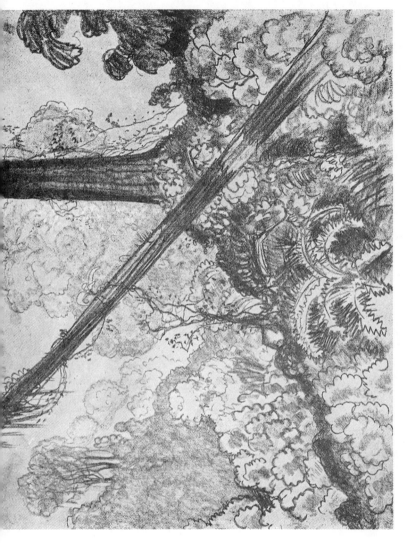

VIRGIN WOOD (*Drawing*)

In the Preanger Regencies, Java

spread miles of the gleaming ricefields. Its wild rush will change to the quiet taskwork as of one who knows there is much to be accomplished throughout the long day; so it slips with a little purr of sound from terrace to terrace of the wide fields, moving slowly now on its unending labour of fructifying the plains.

On another occasion our aim is a crater lake. Again we pass through the deep woods, lichenous, moss grown as those others. No bird breaks the silence. No palms grow at these heights, and nothing would distinguish the woods from those of Europe save for their oppressive monotony of growth, of colour, of everything. It is the antithesis of what the European conceives the East to be. Endless it seems until one ceases to expect change, and is startled almost when after a muddy length of path the lake itself appears in an open space.

The lake. It lies flat and placid in a border of yellow and green rushes: a circle of sky-blue ringed about by oxide green. The bank on the far side rises almost vertically; the trees stand close together, their heads rise over one another rhythmically with the orderliness of a stage decoration, until high above, very high, the colour and the shapes become more vague or disappear when a cloud floats above the silent waters. The decorations of the bank seem petrified; beneath them the waters mirror their pattern, lifeless, unmoving, mysterious. No sound dares to move in the ominous still air.

On other days we see the work in the plantation of the estate; how the bark is stripped from the cut branches, or see along the seed beds where the young shoots appear in the black earth gathered from the virgin woods and covered by glass and ferns as protection against the fierceness of the sun. Or we watch the sorting of the costly seeds, each with a value greater than its weight in gold. Women sit around a frosted glass table in a darkened room; the glass is lighted from below so that an unearthly, pale light strikes upwards on the brown faces bowed over their task, and on the brown hands sorting the seeds one from another with a feather. The colours of their clothing are lost in the gloom; their shapes loom ghostly in the twilit room.

Outside the sun blinds us, and when our eyes grow accustomed again to the glare we see a far crater smoking and determine to visit this during our stay. The day arrived, our host has again provided guides, and as before we climb the steep and slippery paths through

An Artist in the Tropics

the endless, solitary woods. At the crater itself a bare, rugged piece of ground lies before us—a spiral of destruction as though Hell's demons had fought there. From the clefts in the ground smoke comes slowly; the sulphur has yellowed and killed everything. Barren in its corrosion is the mountain which, like a vertical wall, encloses this witch's cauldron. The ground is eaten away, pulverised and undermined by heat and the poisonous gases. All living things have passed away, but high above us the mountains break again into the luxuriant growth of ferns and plants.

Passing between heavy boulders, and straddling a brooklet which breaks across this Dantesque scene, we reach the border of the main crater itself. With each step the ground is hotter. Then the pit is before us. It steams and foams and bubbles—a fury of thick, yellowish-grey pulp from the centre of which a foam of molten lava and poisonous gas sprays out in everlasting war against the solid rock. The poison of the air pricks in one's throat; it is hostile to all live things.

As we look at it we are minded that recent reports have told of craters further East in active eruption. We glance again at this small, less active crater. It is safe, we have been told; it will not change. But as we gaze down into this mysterious lake of molten rock, bubbling, boiling, seething beneath our feet we feel that in this sinister cauldron calamity is brewed in immeasurable potency, which no man can resist or prescribe.

Chapter Ten

The Temple Borobudur

LIKE a magnificent crown, an ancient bronze tiara tarnished only by the passing centuries, the exquisite Borobudur encircles and ennobles the hill-top whereon it stands. Only the volcanoes can vie with it, poised there as it is like eternity brought to shape, towering above the surrounding lands that shrink back in their slightness before such majesty.

On the horizon the enfolding mountain ranges close in the view, their undulating contour broken where the three mighty giants —the Volcanoe Merapi with its everlasting plume of smoke, Mount Merbaboo and Mount Soombing ascend.

Between lies a wide valley, still asleep in the cold light of dawn. Palm crowns seem to float on the dense mists which hang over the ground. No chattering of birds yet disturbs the silence.

Then the flame of the sun rises from behind the mountains. Surya, the Light of Asia itself, shines with its divine light on Buddha, the Enlightened. The innumerable pinnacles of the *stupa* [1] of the enormous temple begin to scintillate, a great shrine of golden filigree. From the unknown highest of the Dhyana-Buddhas, whose domain is zenith, Surya glides slowly down to where the Rulers of the Four Zones of Heaven are enthroned, until at last His radiance illumines the earth, and all the marvellous coronel of the temple sparkles in the life-bringing light. If it were possible for the parts to be fairer than the mighty whole then fairer are the adornments of the Buddhas, Urna, symbol of their divine wisdom.

The silence of the valley resolves itself into a gentle, strange melody, pausing upon the very threshold of sound. Slowly, with

[1]Stupa : An edifice raised to mark a sacred spot or to commemorate some event in the life of a Buddhist Saint.

53

An Artist in the Tropics

each repetition, it becomes more defined. A lonely Hindoo climbs the terraces murmuring prayers as he treads the long, upward road to the Light.

The white mists evaporate before the coming day; the broad valley lands spread fair and far beneath; the palm leaves glitter. On the morning wind a little rumour of life is wafted up from the village.

Of the Borobudur itself what can be said? In its manifold beauty architecture and all that architecture can express reaches its apotheosis, so that one feels that faithfulness to any single one of its many elements would add immeasurable value to the best of our contemporary buildings. Rich beyond power of description in ornament, yet highly monumental; baroque and classical; exuberant and restrained; fragile and massive; severe yet full of mystery; it is the incarnation of the inevitable and eternal, beyond earthly understanding. It is the universe itself symbolised in carven stone.

Obscure is its origin, like the ages which brought it forth. The Javanese régime which fell in the eighth century of our era is lost in the mists of antiquity; forgotten too is the great maritime power which at that time conquered Mid-Java; but here in this phantasmagoria of breathing stone, the spiritual life of those dark powers lives on, and bears its inscrutable witness to their passing. Since the eighth century, when it was built, the temple has borne that witness.

Like jewels in some exquisitely modelled mediæval tiara the Buddhas are set, hundred beyond hundred. Many are damaged, but many more remain seemingly untouched of time. The tempests and earthquakes of a thousand years have left their beauty unimpaired.

Soft, like blossoms, are the mosses which fleck the stones with green and silver-pale loveliness. Far above on the highest terraces glows the symbolled life of eternity. Urging towards it the earthly existence of Buddha is sculptured. Banaspatis guard each gateway to the remoter beyond. Shiva they are, the Devourer of Time, through whom everything passes away into Nirvana reigning above.

" . . . All that lives must die
Passing through nature to eternity."

"The Borobudur, Moonrise" *(Etching)*

The Temple Borobudur

No temple for men, no abode of gods this *stupa* is. It is cosmos itself symbolised: cosmos as a divine plan of transience; cosmos in which everything that is will be dissolved. Every Buddha is a beam of the eternal light radiating across the earthly land. Borobudur is a beacon for all things that are.

Like a tree which fulfils itself with the falling of ripened fruit, Old Java left this richest treasure on the earth. Reverence and care have recently reconstructed it. All about the sacred hill the down-thrown fragments have been set up anew: parts of gateways, over-grown blocks of masonry, a foot, an arm, a hand, each mutilated stone a masterpiece still. Everywhere, too, lie the elaborately carved ornaments, still whole or broken and half-hidden in the rich vegeta-tion. For the greater part of a thousand years time and neglect have had their way at the hill of Borobudur. And far away in the valley the labourer working his field may throw up or bury again one of the ancient, exquisite treasures of the sacred hill.

Chapter Eleven

Borobudur and Tjandi Pawon

THERE is no country without black pages in its history, although by happy dispensation of Providence only history is thus besmirched. Belgium had its Congo, Spain its Holland, Holland its East Indies. Even the greatest apologists for the benefits of the white man to the burden will admit that the activities of the Dutch in the 17th and 18th centuries, as of the Portuguese before them, were marked by no excess of gentleness. The appreciation of the artistic and intellectual values of East Indian culture were a later growth when no longer commercialism was omnipotent.

As one travels now in the East, and, especially in Java, the flood of reaction against the purely material view of exploitation which has held for so long, brings us up against the other extreme. By an amazing swing of the pendulum the arts of Java are exploiting commercialism. The appreciation of native handwoven garments and the art of batik have led the way. Justifiably, for if we needs must love the highest when we see it, the European who could visit Java and neglect its temples, or who did not crave to possess a genuine piece of batik must needs be lost to beauty. But the appreciation of Javanese art has become a cult, and ergo, a commerce. Rubbish for export to meet the demand for the European collecting mania is being produced on a large scale. The Javanese batik wayang puppets on table covers albeit they themselves use neither table covers nor tables, sitting on their hassocks and making the floor their table; they export sixpenny brass Buddhas made by Mahommedans despite the fact that their religion forbids them to represent the human form and even more certainly would forbid them to depict the founder of another religion. But so the business flourishes.

With all this European enthusiasm for the "art" of the East we seem never to have realised that it is essentially inartistic to make

A Buddha, Borobudur *(Drawing)*

Borobudur and Tjandi Pawon

a printed copy of a hand-made batik, and send the spurious imitation to Java. It is but one example of many in the same strain. The Europeans buy native shawls in appreciation of their beauty, whilst the European machines flood the island with the coarsest counterfeits. The natives do not notice the difference, say the cynics; which even if it were true would not morally justify the substitution of unlabelled margarine for genuine butter. As the Dutch government splendidly preserved a work of art of the ancient religion by restoring Borobudur, it would be well if it could exercise its saving grace on behalf of the living art of batik, against which its own peoples are the worst offenders.

As with batik, so also with other forms of Javanese art and their frenzied if indiscriminating admirers. One group would help the musicians with a script of the native music, irrespective of the fact that this has intervals different from ours, is based on rhythm and not on melody, and could reasonably be supposed to be safer in the hands of the Javanese themselves if they desired to write it down.

The same European genius for interference was illustrated for us by the assertions of one person who had become erudite on the matter of the Court dancers. The Sultan of Djocjakarta himself, the Court interpreter, a prince, and other highly placed Javanese assured us that there was no difference between the dancing of the "bedoyos" and that of the "serimpis"—the girls of noble blood and the other court dancing girls; but our European knew better.

Nor are we less humbly acceptive in connection with the fashionable appreciation of architecture shown in Borobudur worship. So many who indulge it have yet to learn that there are two Borobudurs. One is the Borobudur of the Sunday trippers. You have your photograph taken with the temple as adequate background to your superior charms; or even, in a moment of sublime self-assurance, standing in the foreground at the foot of the tree and leaning against the great unfinished Buddha with an arm familiarly thrown around its waist or neck. The folk in Europe are bound to treasure such a photograph!

But when the charming girls and the young men with kodaks have gone, and are enlivening the dull East with a little Western dancing somewhere, the other Borobudur appears and holds sway until Sunday brings the recurring trippers. Through the still

An Artist in the Tropics

evenings Borobudur s ands, moonlit, mysterious, wonderful; through the white mornings a dream of the all-embracing that wears the earth as a jewel of its jewels; through the tropic days "a flame that burns without movement."

"Fine, this Borobudur," our enthusiast gushes, "but you should see the Mendut Temple. That you must see. It is still finer. These big images—magnificent, so imposing they are."

Can a European ever forget to look through European spectacles? In every period of its development European architecture has been essentially the construction of space, whilst in the orient the essential is the creation of the monument, as every *stupa*, and therefore the Borobudur, bears witness. The difference makes the significance of the sacred building a sealed book to the majority of those who come from Northern countries. They walk through the gateways, climb the steps, pass along the galleries, and on the highest terraces they admire the view! Excellent the view is, and worthy of approval, but its admiration helps them to forget that they are in the open all the time, that there is no "inside".

Therefore is it that the Mendut Temple appeals. One not only walks around it but can go inside, and at once one is "at home" again. Images there are—old gods, no doubt—but the thing has some meaning to our practical Western minds. The few who visit the neighbouring little Tjandi Pawon take no interest in it at all, for here you cannot get on top, there is no view, and even though it has an inside there is nothing to look at there.

Still the Pawon, standing like some beautiful field flower in the shadow of the palms and bamboo bushes far below in the valley, or the Borobudur in his stately aloofness, are more to us than the cool, proud Mendut. Or is it merely that the Temple has suffered too much the hand of the restorer?

BOROBUDUR *(Drawing)*

Chapter Twelve

Court Dancers at Djocjakarta

"THE Resident, sir? No, sir, it is quite impossible to get the Resident on the telephone to-day. There is a festival in honour of the Queen's birthday, so. . . ." The voice trailed off with the disconcerting finality peculiar to voices over telephones, but as it was for that very festival that we had dashed by express train to Djocjakarta we were not so easily dismissed.

"That is exactly what we came for," we asserted, and then, before we could pursue the point, the Resident himself was speaking. Little wonder we were thrilled. It would be the first time we would see Java's choreographic art—the fabulous dances concerning which we had heard so much. And your artist is the perfect egoist. Everything which feeds his art will be regarded by him as his by virtue of enthusiasm and what could be more exciting to us than the expectation of the unfolding of this exotic art of Asia in all its beautiful reality within a few hours?

For the Festival at the Resident's house we are expected to come at half-past five, as the Sultan will arrive before six, ere the sun has set bringing to an end the Mahommedan day. When we enter the large front verandah we find many Europeans already forgathered, and every minute brings fresh parties of guests in official or evening dress. On a great lawn, amid rows of Hindoo sculpture, the gloriously coloured and jewelled garments of the natives glitter in the last rays of the sun. They await the arrival of their rulers.

A long procession in strange court attire appears. It is Prince Paku Alam and the Princess with their suite. He is the younger of the two semi-independent rulers at Djocjakarta. His attendants are ranged along one side of the broad semi-circular path leading from the entrance gateway to the front of the house and thence to the

59

An Artist in the Tropics

further gate. The Prince wears a Dutch uniform, but his appearance is not that of a warrior. The quiet, questioning look, from behind gold-rimmed glasses, impresses itself upon us on this occasion as on that later one when we were invited to his palace to see the archives of the Paku Alam family and the priceless collection of ancient weapons and local batik.

A second procession follows. The Sultan, himself, seated in a chariot drawn by many horses, surrounded by footmen who swing great plumes to protect them from the flies. Again the followers take their places along the path, this time at the other side—a brave line, gleaming with tall spears, fantastic with krisses, glinting with gold and jewels. High officials form the immediate suite of the Sultan. His slim figure and finely-modelled princely visage mark him even amid their brilliance. His Javanese head-dress—a carefully folded turban—is adorned with one brilliant diamond, and his general's uniform is also ornamented with precious stones.

Evening falls, and in the brief dusk a myriad servants light the lamps which illuminate the white building and the garden path. Beneath a canopy the Sultan and the Resident take their seats; next to them Prince Paku Alam and the Sultan's Regent have their places, with their courtiers around them. The official reception commences. In long procession the guests pass before the canopy. We greet the Prince; we greet the Resident and his wife; we greet the Sultan, who affably exchanges a few words with us concerning the object of our journey; we greet the Regent. It is but the beginning of official ceremonial. At its heels come many official speeches well beyond the limits of our Malay; official congratulations, toasts and much champagne. Now ribbons of knighthood are proclaimed by the Resident; and, these honours duly bestowed, the Assistant-Resident announces one, the highest distinction we have, for the Resident himself. Highest of all distinctions it may be, but it is nevertheless brought forth from the pocket of the Assistant-Resident, and when the pin will not fasten, a further touch of humanity is given to the ceremony when Madam herself leaves her seat and lends a hand to affix the recalcitrant decoration in her husband's coat.

After that a dance, but not yet the dances for which we wait. Our expectation makes us a little impatient of The Lancers and their successors danced here as at home, save that the tropic heat makes

Court Dancer, Djocjakarta *(Oil painting)*

Court Dancers at Djocjakarta

them less bearable. These ball-room dances seem endless, but at last an open space is cleared in the big hall and the native musical instruments of the "gamelan", the orchestra, are brought in: drums, gongs, metallophones, an Arabian violin, rebab. The players crouch down. The Presentor too sits, and high is the sound of his voice.

And so enchantment. Lightly as though they glide, formal, set, unreal, the magical forms of the bedoyos enter as if in dream. Their looks are fixed, their heads are lifted up, their march is majestic, vibrant, as if this procession of transcendental beings formed part of some holy rite. Like flower petals the gestures slowly expand: exquisite, exotic orchids rather than dance movements. Slowly, holding the action through infinite moments, they will stretch a hand, an arm. More slowly still the whole body passes from poise to poise, and as though by some inward compulsion they move forward in faultless harmony.

The gamelan swells; its waves of sound break and die, to begin anew, pulsing into some other rhythm. Like a glitter of foam upon the wave's surface comes the quick, shrill beat of the brass. With a lightning turn the dancers throw free the silken sampoor fixed at their girdles, and lift it with a fragile gesture of their slim fingers. Sound and movement flows to and fro in perfect unity, even though to the Western ear the shrillness of the women's voices in the orchestra is almost unendurable. Mysterious is the dreamy, unreal music, startling as it suddenly leaps wide intervals of the Eastern scale or slides down in sharp breaks of sound; bizarre it seems, and coloured as some exotic, brilliant bird.

We cannot understand either the language of the Javanese words nor that of the gestures, but the electric atmosphere and intensity of this art enthrals us. How often have we sought it vainly in the theatres of sophisticated Europe. Excellence of technique we may have found in our own country, but too often its tawdry surface brilliance with which the executant hypnotises his public is but a veil behind which artist and public alike can disguise their vacuity. Here in the cloister-like seclusion of the Javanese palace an art full of significance and perfect in its presentation continues untouched and unspoiled. Here gleams still the refinement of the old Asiatic aristocracy, and when the dancers have disappeared, gathered back as it were to the secret source whence they emanated, their essence remains like a strange perfume on the Eastern night.

Chapter Thirteen

Visitors' Day at the Palace, Djocjakarta

To see the Kraton, the Palace of the Sultan! A palace of the Arabian Nights, nay, a veritable town of palaces the Kraton must be, and now this fairy tale of the Orient is to become reality. We shall enter the mighty gateways, where sentinels, immobile and aloof in their task, guard the Holy; we shall cross courtyards shadowed by high waringin trees, and the palace walls will close in the silence, secretly, majestically, grandly. In this maze of apartments and buildings the inhabitants are counted by thousands. There beats the heart of Javanese music, lives the gamelan, the forgers, the wayang both as shadow show and acted, and also the finest dancing of the noble serimpis and bedoyos. Imposing Pendoppos[1] will we find in gardens full of flowers. . . . But now the imagination pauses, for where, in the omnipresent green which the East proved itself to be, especially in the dry season, would we find the riches of blossom with which we had invested those courts? Reluctantly we abandon the vision of an Oriental Versailles or Hampton Court, but still we cling to the thought that the gateway to Ancient Java is to open for us. Up then, to see the Kraton, the Palace of the Sultan.

"The omnibus leaves at a quarter to nine, sir."

"——?!"

"The omnibus of the Hotel. It is the easiest way to get there, or you must. . . ."

Whatever the alternative is we bow to the conventional method, and the omnibus accordingly it is. Thus to see the Kraton proves to begin: being brought to the Resident's office with other tourists; secondly: waiting until more sheep flock to this unromantic fold;

---

[1]Pendoppo: open audience hall, with a high roof on wooden pillars, and without walls.

A Javanese *(Oil painting)*

Visitors' Day at the Palace

and finally, at a stroke of the clock, the official appears who is to guide the polyglot company, and away we go. By omnibus!

At last we stop before the Kraton itself. Here watchmen stand, with long lances, in the official court dress, the bunched-up sarong, the Javanese jacket, the curling plait. We enter the wide aloon-aloon, the forecourt, and the heterogeneous crowd of us stare at the heterogeneous pile of buildings. The old cannons sleep. The guide explains things in Dutch, which pleases us because since his father and his father's father were also in the Kraton as servants to the late Sultan he may know more about it than the English-speaking Hindoo from a hotel who has constituted himself guide to a dozen Americans. This gentleman's explanations sparkle with humour; and when we compare his English stories with those of the Dutch rival to which we listen with our other ears, we decide that the strange narratives of the old Buddhism or the more piquant details of life at the Kraton are as speculative as the European exchanges on after-war finance.

The long pilgrimage through the buildings has not the saving grace of humour, nor of beauty. Dilapidation, oriental neglect and carelessness everywhere, and the poorest set of buildings we have set eyes upon. Not even picturesque disorder reigns. In a crude shed which looks like a stable to the European eye, we see— the Sultan's gamelan, and in a corner a heap of gold payongs[1] and spears.

Another door: the state coaches, of which the finest are covered with rather perished canvas. The mustiness of a cellar-atmosphere mixes with incense smoke which servants prepare continually from the burning of coco-fruit peel. Then again gardens, great courts with palm plants in majolica pots.

A single fine pendoppo, disgraced by European paraffin lamps and equally vulgar armchairs with curly legs and plush covers, is the next attraction. Thank heaven all this is doomed. The present Sultan, Hamengku Buwono VIII, has a project for restoring everything in Javanese style, and the execution of his plans has commenced. The lamps will disappear from the beautifully carved, gilded, and painted ceiling, and, indeed, when we visited the hall subsequently, the hideous chairs had already gone.

[1] Payong: umbrella; also emblem of dignity, gilt wholly or partially according to the rank of noble .

An Artist in the Tropics

Here and there servants linger, servants "who only stand and wait", it would seem. Or are they there to keep an eye upon the visitors? They examine each other's hair without the least embarrassment, they chatter and whisper; further on women sit giggling and playing cards; to the stranger under the sidelong scrutiny of these many eyes the atmosphere seems full of intrigue. We are shown the banqueting hall where three hundred guests can sit; and also we see the wall against which in the old days sentenced criminals were stabbed. In front of it is a raised place where the seated Sultans exercised their particular privilege of watching these

spectacles. The guide's flow of humour is in full flood at this point; tipping time is getting near.

At many corners watchmen stand with lances, but the points are cased in leather. Others have a rifle, but it is some sort of harmless, old civic-guard's weapon. The sentinel is so unconcerned with his that it rests against a specially erected wooden stand. Two captains of the watch on their hassocks converse intimately over a cup of tea. Polonius gossips with Polonius. Five servants sit behind them.

Stairs, walls and courts with caged birds precede the spectacle of the Sultan's elephant. He stands under a roof with one foreleg tied so closely to a big pole that he cannot move it other than by shoving around the pole. That is what he does now, therefore;

Visitors' Day at the Palace

to-day, to-morrow, the day after to-morrow. Once a week, on Saturdays, he has his day off; he is taken for an airing and allowed to bathe in the brook. But to-day is not Saturday, and so he stands pathetically and shoves round as he will do for many years until the rope has worn this pole almost through, as it has worn one near by.

A new guard arrives, parades past with slow pace; dull grey-heads, goodly bespectacled little men with a plait coming from under the head-dress. They also carry and put aside the lances with their leather sheaths; they also sit down quietly, they also chat listlessly and commence to drink tea.

The elephant propels itself around its pole endlessly. . . .

Round a corner we stay behind; we are permitted to, says our guide. We yearn for the aloon-aloon, for space and open air, and delivery from this oppressive silence. True, the great court is a bare, dusty desert, but the wide-spreading waringin trees cut to shape are protecting payongs outstretched above the balustrades which surround them; emblems, it is said, of the protective power of the Sultan and as exalted as he. They make the enormous space look majestic, but they cannot obliterate the impression of the realities of the Kraton as we have seen it.

In spite of all it is here that the culture of Java still lives and blooms unseen, as, unseen by the casual visitor, the old tree still brings forth its blossoms. How many branches it has lost in the passing of time, but its flowers are still pure and princely, and such as have not thrived for centuries in any Occidental court. The dance, the wayang, the gamelan and the batik remained, though the ruler's secular power decayed. No longer may he lead his armies; no longer stately ambassadors move in imposing procession across the now empty aloon-aloon. Years have elapsed since the last building was added to the intricate structure of the Kraton; now, scarcely any attempt is made to repair the ravages of decay; mildew, moss, dirt or weeds gather on the perishing wood and crumbling stone. For many ages the energy of the people was spent within the Kraton's walls; intellectually and materially all possessions of the people were vested in the Ruler, that truly Eastern Potentate. And for ages the whims and caprices of that All-Mighty One dissipated the wealth, until at last even his bullying servants could no longer extort money from his subjects, could no longer levy tribute upon the impoverished

An Artist in the Tropics

and exhausted mass of the people. The Shiva made room for the submissive Mohammedanism, and the servile attitude towards the All-Destroying God changed later into the submissiveness of the slave to the divinely empowered king, to whom year after year tribute in full measure was paid without question and without thought of injustice.

Now the free energy of the people has died, but with it too has gone the power of these tyrants who for so long lived as parasites on their subjects. Even the show of power, the ancient decorum and greatness of gesture, are but the pale shadow of what they have been.

Around the palace walls live the population in extreme poverty. Such dejection is not found in the islands outside the Principalities. For although the wild, seafaring Madura population, the Batak of the Sumatra highlands, and the Dajak of Central Borneo live in little better condition, it seems with them to be rather their natural and primitive existence, lightly and carelessly led. Here, however, the old oppression still marks the mien of the people.

Nevertheless, and in spite of all their antiquated social arrangements and wide-spread poverty, the Principalities have a culture and a refinement of race, and of the arts which remind one of the artistic efflorescence of the Medici, a culture which subtly penetrates all classes of society, a culture more valuable than material welfare, and one such as Europe has not known for centuries, whilst its art has become increasingly a stranger in its own land.

It is thus that the visitor sees the Kraton on Fridays, and thus he muses there. For the Kraton on a visitors' day is a stage seen in daylight, emptied of its actors and its accessories. One evening the still scene shall live anew for us. We have been invited to assist at the exercise of the dancing girls. Our carriage halts where the street ends against the high wall, we enter the great gate opening on the wide, dark courtyard. A single, solitary lamp gleams in the black silence, and soon we stand before the main gate, where left and right the watchmen are posted under small pendoppos. We show our invitation and are permitted to pass. The dimly lighted pathway brings us to another high, dark gateway, its gate closed. When one of the watchmen gently knocks the heavy door slowly swings ajar; a whisper passes to and fro; quietly the door closes again. The watchman explains that someone within has gone to inform the

66

Visitors' Day at the Palace

Sultan's brother of our coming. We wait on in the darkness, and after a little while the gate is slowly opened again. Permission has been given for us to pass. When the door has fully opened we see in the dim, vague light of a little lamp the watchmen behind it with their huge, drawn swords and Javanese spears, their shadows gigantic on the white walls. We follow our guide, and soon from a large pendoppo a black silhouette appears against the lights behind, and the Sultan's brother, Pangeran Hadisooryo, welcomes us and bids us follow him. Across the marble floor, shining under the lights of lamps, chairs and tables have been placed for the European visitors.

At our left the instruments of the gamelan stand and wait; nothing else breaks the clear expanse of the wide floor. In the darkness outside rustles the rain. Now, noiselessly on their bare feet, some of the players come like shadows in the dim light, and crouch on their hassocks behind their instruments. Simultaneously from our right, crouching as they creep forward, the dancers appear; phantasmal. No noise disturbs the utter silence. The sarong they wear pulled up high under the arms so that it leaves the shoulders and arms bare; they wear no ornamental trimmings. The smallest and youngest, children still, remain at the extreme right, but in the centre of the hall, close to where we have taken up our position, the four serimpi dancers crouch, pale and yellow in the golden light of the lamps against the dark brown and gilt of the wooden wainscoting. Now the gamelan begins, and all the dancers rise and sway to and fro with the soft music, wherein it seems the rustling of tropic leaves is interwoven with the murmur of rain.

Who has heard a bird begin to sing in the dead stillness of a summer night before the dawn appears? Some decisive notes lightened and made lovely by a first essay of swift sound, then an echo from afar, till the long tones repeat from every side, and suddenly, again, again another bird will take up the strain, pouring out his own bright cascade of clear, music. Thus the gamelan begins, and in perfect unity with its rhythm the arms of the dancers rise and fall like palm leaves stirred by the dawn breeze. Their hands write strange hieroglyphics on the air, like necromancers conjuring unearthly spirits, slowly following the flowing lines of some secret and ethereal script.

After a while the fine fingers draw the dagger, the Javanese kriss which they each wear like some exotic stamen at their girdles.

An Artist in the Tropics

Crouching servants hand over shields, but both these and the weapons are of buffalo leather, explains the Pangeran who sits at our sides, so that the dancers cannot harm one another. Later, in the same highly conventionalised way, they handle pistols, always as though they were plucking and presenting flowers. No change of expression enlivens the still faces. What thoughts, we wonder, drift and die behind the lowered eyelids?

When, after a while, we chat with the Pangeran and ask him amusedly whether the pistols are charged and meant for us, he abandons his official demeanour for a time, and laughs heartily and drinks our health light-heartedly in the Tokayer, the wine which has been brought in the meantime in true court fashion by a long, silent, obsequious procession of servants. And so the human East dispels our dream.

THE WATER CASTLE (*Drawing*)

Chapter Fourteen

The Water Castle, Djocjakarta

GONE is the greatness of the Water Palace of the Sultans of yore, crumbled its stone. Earthquakes have shaken it to ruins, and over its fallen masonry moss and vegetation have grown in tropic luxuriance. Débris only is left of the mass of the great halls, the stairs, the corridors; a musty smell of dampness and decay is over all; but the magic and grandeur of this old home of the Potentates lingers yet. A guide shows us what was once the oratory of the Sultan, a divan with a cooling curtain of falling water closing off a small apartment, a children's bathing pond over which palms wave. The larger square ponds are surrounded by massive pots in which once a variety of flowers were grown, but now only weeds and the wind-sown seeds thrive there.

Yonder must have been the orchards. Now they are a tangle of banana trees, coconut palms and wild vegetation. Among them, here and there, stand some plain wooden houses, but everything seems forgotten and empty and dead. The large ponds, in which stagnant water remains, are covered with duckweed and over-grown with plants, so that in the still water no building, tree, nor sky is reflected.

Then in the solitude of the fairy castle voices sound from afar, and a few moments later the ancient, royal ponds are invaded by infant, modern Java. Plop! Plop! The brown little bodies, with ball-round rice-bellies, jump in. One tiny person soaps his laundry, and of the foaming lather the bathers each get a lick on their little heads. Now they dive and swim, and in the rhythm of their movements they resurrect the inherent rhythm of their race. A little fellow of some eight years splashes and slaps the water with a flat, stretched hand, until the tinkling cascade of the sounds of the gamelan are evoked in a lively pithy cadence beneath his childish palm. Does

An Artist in the Tropics

he imitate, or was it thus by chance the gamelan was born? Deep, dull thuds of sound he makes, miraculously bronze-like and sombre, and intermittently the bright, clean music of the little fountains that spring up around him complete the theme. Leaping and striking with full force he succeeds in evoking the middle tones of his scale until the whole gamut is his.

And, like a little faun strayed from ancient days, he dances there, with streaks of green duckweed garlanding body and brown head.

COOLIES RESTING (Oil painting)

Chapter Fifteen

The Living Ornament

GONE is the glory of the Water Palace, ruined its plaster ornaments, though the design of these still lives in the primeval, eternal folk art which outlives stone.

No Sultan, princess or haughty concubine strides now through these gardens. No high officials, no messengers, no armourers nor gardeners tread here now, however many passed to and fro in the old days. But in the now empty and unguarded gateways, where once the watchmen kept vigil in this place of kings, the village girls batik the old ornament on their sarongs.

In a corner behind the great gateway we find by accident the fallen leaves gathered together. Here the children play. When we come they shyly run away, but they leave behind in the thick layer of the grey street-dust a wayang figure exquisitely drawn with the finger tip or piece of wood. Fluently the curved line burgeons into ornament, stately and grand, moving intangibly like a shadow along a wall, at once majestic and whimsical. Nothing, nothing can preserve this transient beauty of line. When we go it is soon trodden into oblivion or blown away by the wind. Yet we need not fear. The ornament which speaks to us from the grey dust lives on immaterially. It is immortal in the immortal race; reincarnate in every individual Javanese; lasting while the nation lasts.

Chapter Sixteen

Painting in the Kraton, Djocjakarta

To wear evening dress as early as ten a.m., to sit for an hour and a half on a settee with a Sultan and converse with him in Malay when one knows only a few score words of the language: it would be difficult to say whether physical heat or nervous tension were the outstanding sensation of my first ceremonial visit to the Kraton at Djocjakarta.

At the first gate I show my card of invitation to the sentinel; at the second I hand it over to the officer, who, surrounded by the guard with long lances, shows the way.

Sitting on a front verandah I perceive the Sultan and with him his brother, the Pangeran Hadisooryo. I bow, and as I pause near them both rise graciously to receive me. Then, when the Sultan stretches out his hand, I dare approach. The Sultan points to the left as though for me to be seated there, and immediately my difficulties begin. Where am I to sit? The chair where his brother has been seated seems out of the question; and the only other place being the settee alongside the Sultan himself is equally dubious as etiquette. There is an empty chair away on the other side, but that is obviously not indicated. My brain rapidly makes a chess problem of the matter: four squares and three pieces with white to move and win. If I make a bad move it causes me not only to cut a poor figure at the moment, but may jeopardise my chance of being permitted to paint in the Kraton. Nor is there time for thought, for it is impossible to remain standing when the Sultan has indicated his wish that I shall sit. But he himself has sensed my hesitation, and as I commence to formulate a question in Malay which I speak with such difficulty his quick gesture anticipates my query. I share the settee.

Painting in the Kraton, Djocjakarta

Now again the Sultan sits; next to him the Pangeran takes his chair, and between them I seat myself, my dull black evening clothes stiff and orthodox against their loose, richly-coloured Javanese garments adorned here and there with glittering pins and diamonds.

Eight or more servants on their hassocks sit near. No Javanese stands in the presence of his ruler. They bring cigars, cigarettes, tinders; they carry little tables and give each of us one; they offer cool drinks. When I commit myself to speech whilst my glass is being filled, and say something like "Berhenti"[1] instead of the word which for the moment escapes my memory, the Sultan politely inquires whether I ask for brandy. My host, however, rapidly realises that my Malay is not one of my best accomplishments, and when we lift our glasses it is innocent lemonade which glitters in them.

The Sultan orders the accessories of the wayang performance to be brought, and presents me with the programme of a performance which has lasted through four successive days. He presents me with photographs of it, and accords me permission to paint in the Kraton, promising to arrange for the Court dancers to sit for me. We speak of the garments of the wayang actors, and of the imitation batik as we print it in Holland.

"It is very coarse," I comment.

"As a rule, yes; but I have seen beautiful ones also," says the Sultan politely. I wonder whether he knows that one of the blackest sins of our European life is that we can hardly make any intrinsically beautiful thing now because we have sold ourselves to imitation and counterfeit. That is the curse of the Occident: we can make our imitations so perfect that practically nobody can tell whether he has the genuine or the spurious thing. As I sit on the Sultan's settee I have a moment's vision of the poor wretches who, in all the big European museums, copy the fine woven and embroidered ornament of antiquity with meticulous care for large-scale factory reproduction, stifling every chance of original feeling which might have been in these doomed draughtsmen breathing the centrally-heated air of the museums. All this for the sake of making "cheap" goods— cheap, the axis around which everything in our Western world turns, accepting the basic falseness of it all without scruple.

My thoughts return to the immediate present as the gamelan begins to play, and my host explains that the actors are going to

[1] Berhenti : " Stop " ; used, however, only as to carriages, etc., and not as I did here.

An Artist in the Tropics

rehearse, and invites me to watch the rehearsal. When eventually I take my leave an appointment has been made for the first day when I shall paint in the Kraton.

Again a carriage brings me to the Kraton, again I cross the wide courtyard closed in by walls and set with numerous pendoppos, pass the many sentinels, regents with their followers, orderlies. Chairs and a table have been placed in readiness. When the canvas is put on the easel and the colourbox opened, the Pangeran immediately orders that a small table shall be fetched to accommodate it; it must not be left on the ground.

In the silence of the front verandah the Pangeran takes his seat. Then, unheard, barefooted on the smooth marble, a slender, almost transcendental form, appears the dancer, tall, straight and slowly moving. Two women servants, humbly crouching, accompany her. They all make the gesture of homage called "sembah"[1] for the Prince, after which the thin hands are spread open like flower petals, the fingers frail and articulated like some perfect growth of bamboo.

I bow. All are silent; only the dancer's own language of gesture has passed by way of greeting.

"Does the Raden Adyeng[2] speak Malay?" I ask the Pangeran. His reply being in the negative causes any request as to pose or rest to go through his translation, for I do not know one word of Javanese. Dead silence again.

The dancer seems a vision from the Arabian Nights. Her face is strangely yellow under her gold diadem; it is set in black ornament of painted hair, conventional, mask-like. Lustrous black is the brow, and pink the gently wavering line which surrounds the eye, of which the white also is tinted; the lips are blood red. A white feather rises high above the diadem; the heavy black coiffure is sparkling with small white flowers and three large ones of the colour of the jacket, whilst high around the dark hair glitter and sway five flowers in exquisite filigree on quivering gold stems.

In the still heat the colours too, for all their brilliance, seem hushed into silence. A soft, greenish haze from the plants outside tones

---

[1]Sembah : A gesture of both hands put together and lifted in front of the face, the head being slightly bowed.

[2]Raden Adyeng : Noble Title.

COURT DANCER, DJOCJAKARTA *(Oil painting)*

Painting in the Kraton, Djocjakarta

down their primitive vividness, the marble floor reflects pale lights which cast iridescent colours across the unshadowed face.

Nobody speaks save for an occasional whisper. Then through the almost palpable silence a harsh shriek breaks from some exotic bird, many of which are caged down in the walled inner garden. Like some strange bird also, lovely in the daring beauty of brilliant plumage, the poised serimpi stands.

Yonder, the marble floor of the great banqueting hall, the golden hall, Bangsal Kentjono, is being polished by some thirty unheard working servants. A little beyond, others are busy with gold and paint working upon the carved timber of the pillars. Now and again a knocking from above breaks across the quietude. After, silence again reigns, as in some cloistered garden.

Suddenly the Pangeran slips down from his chair and crouches down beside it; his soft whisper ceases; the Sultan comes. Quickly he draws near; erect of stature, free of stride, he moves unheard, barefooted, across the floor. He talks to the gilders, the woodcarvers, and his sentences are punctuated by their respectful "inggeh"[1] as they make the gesture "sembah". Also to the servants polishing the floor the Sultan pays attention, and again their "inggeh", "inggeh" is heard. He passes along the hedge of plants in great pots; I bow as he approaches, and he greets me before he enters his bureau.

At another time he comes to look at the picture which so occupies the foreigner, seeking so earnestly among his European pigments for the strange sheen and glitter of this Javanese colouring. The Sultan would not be a Javanese Prince did he not make some courteous remark.

"Modern picture" he says quizzingly in Dutch.

Strange it must look to him in this country which itself has no art of painting. But the artist who wrestles with the problems of his painting has little time to muse. The intense heat dries the colours and quickly tires the model, who suddenly, after a "sembah", sinks down for a while. Little wonder, for the few hours of the sitting have been preceded by three hours of dressing, arranging the hair, the flowers, the painted face, winding the sarong around the slender waist, fastening it with the metal girdle wherein the kriss, the dagger, rests.

[1]Inggeh : " Yes ".

75

An Artist in the Tropics

How strange must appear the impedimenta of the artist to his onlookers! Some children, little naked ones, steal near secretly, and peer through the bushes with bright eyes. An easel that folds together and unscrews; a canvas stretched like a drum skin; the wide brushes; the palette where the thumb peeps through; these things are magic. But best of all are the tubes which gush forth the fierce red or clear white. One or two of them, and sometimes a woman servant crouches nearer still to perceive more clearly these foreign happenings.

Gradually the whispers grow into lively conversation. Easy speech swells into bursts of sound, soft laughter into occasional wild outbursts. But the dancer stands immobile, unchanged, imperturbable; nothing varies in her unmoving face until the work comes to an end.

Chapter Seventeen

The Susuhunan Receives

GAREBEG BESAR at Solo. Festival day and audience at the court of the Susuhunan, Paku Buwono, who is the Nail which holds the World; the Tenth. Indeed, a great one on earth is he. A living monument of his own supreme kingliness he strides on; slowly, imposingly. Massively his garments spread as he seats himself upon his gold throne.

He is the Ruler; to the tips of his fingers he is the Oriental King, and far flash the lightnings of the enormous carbuncle in his ring. Rings, rather; for on every finger they shine, so that his hands, resting on either knee, glitter like crowns. Black is his Javanese jacket, cut to the old style, short in the back where the dagger is thrust in the girdle, long points hanging down in front. It is firmamented with jewels and decorations numberless. White is the high transparent official head-dress, the kuluk; violet is the girdle; brown the narrow, kilt-like sarong, and wonderfully ornamented with the royal pattern; blue and red exquisitely interwoven the silk of the trousers above the scarlet-stockinged feet in their black slippers trimmed with gold.

Around him the world of his followers is but a wider garment of his glory. In the dust of the ground everybody crouches, even his sons. There, bowed on their hassocks, sit his regents whose garments are embroidered with gold. There are his spear-men, his archers, his guards; a little farther on men with rifles, with swords, with krisses. Numberless are the courtiers and servants. One group of his guards in bright, fierce-green jackets, another in flame red, vie in shouting their respect to the Sultan—strophe and antistrophe of homage to the High One. Later the riflemen will take their turn with a volley of salute.

An Artist in the Tropics

Nor must his glory alone be satisfied with so much honour; the Ruler must also be amused. Two dwarfs have followed in his train, and the Mighty One has his blind men and wild animals. Gamelans play for him: orchestras at the right, orchestras at the left, touching lightly or drumming terribly on their instruments. The dignified chords of the ancient Dutch National Anthem arise from numerous trumpets; and yonder, fiercely and penetratingly, Javanese bamboo flutes play a native melody. Drums, flutes, trumpets and all else make simultaneous tumult, blended only in the echoes from the walls of the surrounding buildings. Who but the Sunan could have so much music played at the same time?

Behind the Susuhunan are scores of women anointed with the borèh, applied on official feasts only. They kneel and hold all possible ensigns and emblems of dignity, displayed according to the ancient Javanese custom and law, the "Adat". They carry shields of purest gold, many swords, straight and curved, poniards set with pearls and encrusted with valuable stones, ornamented and adorned lances, javelins and long spears, heavy and strong, a gold elephant and gold ornaments, the Sunan's gold sirih service, the Sunan's gold spittoon.

Everything should be of gold, the noblest of metals. For holy is the Sunan, higher in rank than a Sultan; and holy everything that is His. The ordinary folk will gladly bargain for a small bottle of the water in which he bathed, certain cure as it is for their illnesses. When he has chewed the sirih-mixture, the lump will be kneeled for. With the All-Highest nothing can be low.

Did not even the Sultan of Djocjakarta kneel once a year at the throne of this highest Potentate who has ever trodden the earth since, in remote ages, lived the Emperors of Mataram whose descendant the Sunan is; and has not this immemorial salute been cleverly metamorphosed by his arriving in the military uniform of a Dutch General now? In truth the power of the Sunan must know no diminution.

As the Sunan seats himself, volley after volley is discharged thunderingly from the rifles. The leaves flutter down from the shaken trees. Then the great guns out-thunder even the rifles. A train of courtiers draws near. They are slender as the wayang-puppets, as slowly-moving and as mysterious. Foot by foot they advance, wave upon wave of homage, towards their Sunan. Or a few will sit on their hassocks facing the throne, and shifting forward

An Archer of the Guard, Solo *(Oil painting)*

The Susuhunan Receives

on these enter the pendoppo making the prayer-like gesture of honour, called the "sembah", three times as they make each movement. It takes time, but what is time to the Ruler? Can anything exist save for his honour? The courtiers halt at last at their Emperor's feet, bowing their heads, folding their hands, the ancient attitude, "silo", of one who would express reverence and modesty. One now addresses his master in the metaphorical tongue of the Court, the high-Javanese which is spoken to a person of high rank, to which the distinguished one replies in the entirely different low-Javanese.

The Sunan utters a command. A long procession approaches, carrying high structures of bamboo with presents to the multitude from the Ruler. Adorned with brightly coloured flags appear piles of fruit, eggs and confectionery, towers of dainties carried by hundreds of the court servants. All the royal gifts are composed to form ornaments; beautiful as well as useful must be this gesture from the Palace to the people. Slowly the long procession passes out by the main gate.

Under a gold umbrella, sign of the highest dignity, a glass is being brought in for the Sunan, and the servants wait attentively. Men on their hassocks bring in a table covered with cloth of gold and place upon it some object hidden from us by yet another golden cloth. A slight movement of the Ruler's hand, and a bowl of gold is revealed filled with holy flowers which are now being presented to the distinguished guests.

Next to the Sunan sits simply the Resident. He is called The Ruler's Elder Brother. He drinks the Sunan's health, hailing him by a row of titles of terrifying length—such length that the Resident has perforce to read them from a paper in his hand. The Ruler responds and drinks his Elder Brother's health with becoming dignity.

And I, witnessing all this—and I, describing all this, am but an artist from a far country. I have no gold nor servants, nor daggers; no ornaments nor thickly encrusted jewels; no rich attire. My very best dress I have on, or rather the very best suit of an official who loaned his to me as he had to appear in his official robes, and my own evening clothes are left behind in a trunk at Surabaya. No lounge suit would avail me on such an occasion. Only in evening dress are Europeans admitted; his Highness desires that we all

An Artist in the Tropics

appear in this most absurd of all our garments with its ludicrous suggestion of parts accidentally cut away by some naughty child. Here then I stand in the prescribed attire, a coat among the other coats; all of us, blue-ish or black, spick and span or shabby, too fully or too tightly cut, we flutter our opulent or worn tails with Occidental decorum, a poor drab thing enough in face of this slow-moving, elaborate ritual of the coloured East.

COURT DANCER WITH ARROW, SOLO *(Etching)*

Chapter Eighteen

The Artist in the Kraton, Solo

BOWING, the nephews of the Susuhunan of Solo, the highest of Java's Sultans, receive us at the gate. Raden Mas Hario Atmodjo and Raden Mas Ngabehi Atmosapootro are their melodious names, and their appearance is worthy of them: the upper part of their bodies is bare, a beautiful gold sword is in the girdle at the front and a graceful kriss at the back, the sarong is drawn up high as the Kraton custom is. To a Dutch artist, who is accustomed to being the butt of the small pebbles and errant cherry stones of the youth of his own nation, the contrast of this reception is rather an arresting beginning. A further contrast is afforded by the aloon-aloon. This should be a stately entrance to the great palace, but in spite of the majestic waringin trees it shows in the dry season as a desert of ashy, volcanic sand, and in the rainy half-year as an enormous quagmire of mud. But whatever its condition, solemnly and with the tranquillity which lifts the great ones of the earth above haste, princes and regents, each followed by six or eight servants in silent queue, stride across it with dignity. The servants are needed to carry such impedimenta as might conceivably be required, if conception can stretch to lances in leather cases, a gold box, a silver tray, a magnificent dagger; but at least they will serve the purpose of enhancing the splendour of the head of the procession.

How modest the man of the West must seem to them. He is not followed by a single servant, but in spite of himself, his arrival is translated into Javanese processional. As soon as the carriage stops some of the watch possess themselves of his implements and follow him in the prescribed way. One solemnly carries the artist's easel, paint bespattered though it be, as if it were a sword of honour encrusted with precious stones; another has taken possession of

An Artist in the Tropics

the colour box, whilst a third lifts up the canvas on its stretcher as if it were the Susuhunan's own gold payong. Thus accompanied we enter the great gateway called Kori Talangpaten in a manner worthy of the court. With three followers I have a sufficient retinue to be introduced to the Susuhunan's sons, who now draw near, Pangeran Koosoomo Yoodo and Pangeran Hadiwidyoyo, and their fluent Dutch makes conversation easy for me.

The person who is to sit for me this morning will be ready shortly; would I care to look round meantime?

We pass through gateways and across courtyards. The corridors are lined with guards; my guides inform me that on the one side are the military, on the other the civic watch. Portraits of His Highness are shown to me: here as a youth, there with his wife. We pass row upon row of cupboards containing the innumerable dishes of the ordinary and the gala dinner services, but the young courtier's enthusiasm kindles rather for the weapons. Native ones alternate with foreign. Long lines of rifles, shining bundles of bayonets, lances, spears, krisses and swords, parade swords and scimitars, pistols and revolvers both plain and inlaid, damaskenes, an antique blunderbuss with a brass barrel which resembles a trumpet, modern folding guns; a long sword of genuine Toledo steel of which the keen point can be curved back to the hilt as if it were a flower stem; an air gun which, in honour of the visitor, is discharged; brilliant helmets with mighty eagles upon them, bullet-proof cuirasses, arrows with barbed hooks on springs, gigantic clubs—there seems no end of the armoury. One would have thought that here were enough weapons to depopulate the globe, but the folding gun has given me a nostalgia for my folding easel . . . how far from it have we wandered, I wonder. Now we come to a room full of Beaumont rifles, multitudinous muzzle-loaders and breech-loaders and at last, to my relief, there comes an end to the show of weapons.

Now we may escape to our painting. But no. We must climb the tower and enjoy the view over the Kraton gardens and buildings. On the highest platform is the divine region where the Goddess of the South Seas comes and visits the Susuhunan of Solo occasionally; there is no admittance for lesser visitors there. On the penultimate gallery is the little room where visitors are requested to sign their names, after which one is shown round the balcony from which the view includes the entrance roads coming together in an obtuse angle

Court Dancer, Solo *(Oil painting)*

The Artist in the Kraton, Solo

and named Soopit Oorang—claws of a crawfish—after this shape. Yonder is the house of the Ruler's first wife, the Ratoo Mas, and beyond it the great banqueting pendoppo. Away on the horizon stand the three mighty volcanoes, Mount Lawoo, Soombing, and ever-smoking Merapi.

After the descent of the tower I am really brought to the pendoppo where the crouched orchestra awaits the dancers, and after a little further delay work is actually begun amid a wide circle of spectators who have been lured by the preparations. One courtier inquires whether the "photo" is to be done in colours. The artist starts.

A few minutes later the hoot of a motor horn betokens an interruption, though hardly six lines are yet on the canvas. A brother of the Ruler has arrived, accompanied by his eldest son. The followers, with various symbols of their dignity, pass by, only their masters stay awhile wondering what the white man is about.

The white man tries to work as if nothing were happening.

Before the procession has completely retired a new one files in; it seems as if the white walls themselves have opened to emit it. On his thin hand, bent backwards to an extent which is miraculous to the Occidental, a servant carries a gold tray bearing a beverage; a second servant follows carrying a gold payong majestically; a file of women servants follow with shuffling feet, pausing only for a cursory glance in our direction.

A troop of the guard marches on. Scarlet is the jacket and the head-dress from which three flaps hang as though they dripped blood. The men fetch halberds and spears, pass by again to render honour and homage to the Sunan.

Hardly has the last of the watch passed when a blind man comes, fumbling, feeling with his stick and followed by several others. Once these poor creatures were palace servants; now that their disease has made them unfit for further service they enjoy the Ruler's charity and in return amuse him with their wit, grimaces and pranks. Later they come back from their miserable duty, and again the file of their dead, mask-like faces passes slowly on.

The artist tries to notice nothing but to concentrate on his painting. Apart, however, from these constantly passing processions, some thirty spectators have gathered about him, and none of his movements or gestures escape their devoted attention. These are seated on his right; on his left an even more numerous group

An Artist in the Tropics

forgathers. And behind the nephews of the Susuhunan sit and chat quietly together whilst their servants attend them with cigarettes and lemonade.

The Sunan's secretary now arrives and has a conversation in Malay with the queer visitor from the Western world. He wears the court headgear, the high kuluk, a cone-shaped symbol of high office, and our next visitor also proclaims his exalted station by a like outward and visible sign.

The artist pauses in choosing a new brush. A carriage halts at the gateway and throngs of servants and courtiers run to it. It brings the Ruler's youngest children who return from the morning lessons at school. Six girls they are, in European check dresses and straw hats, from beneath which they lift their amazed faces to regard this strange man and his stranger doings in their courtyard.

Many servants follow them, with a half-naked boy carrying a gold payong at the last. They all sit down for a while to enjoy fully this unexpected change in their cloistered lives of monotony.

The artist makes a supreme effort at concentration. He cleans a corner of his palette and puts on some fresh colour. The tube, flashing in the fierce light like a little mirror, squelches forth the wet, soft paint, and immediately all the children shout and cheer and scream with laughter, tumbling about in their mirth when with a few strokes a watchman at the gate has been recognisably sketched.

The more the painting progresses the more difficult it becomes to see it well in the wall-less pendoppo with lights and reflection coming upon it from every side. The artist brings his easel outside to get the full light, makes a few steps backward, when the wind, which all the morning has been blowing gently but nevertheless enough to worry, comes in a sudden gust and sends easel and canvas to the ground.

The next day he has gathered all his energy to face his task again. Before he has begun the Susuhunan himself arrives and takes stately possession of the next pendoppo. His gamelan-players begin to sound the fragile tones which tinkle through the morning air. His Highness wants to amuse himself with the dancing of the court-girls. Exquisite and slender they move to and fro like flowers on wind-touched stems, and high on his gold seat the Ruler sits in state.

COURT DANCER, SOLO *(Etching)*

The Artist in the Kraton, Solo

When the end of the artist's working time arrives, His Highness beckons, and servants, humbly crouching with the big canvas, carry it past the gazing, bent gamelan-players and hold it high for the inspection of their Prince. He indicates with a single finger: a little closer, now turn a fraction, thus. Almighty in his pose he examines the progress of the work.

Chapter Nineteen

A Wayang Performance in the Mangkoonegaran

THE Mangkoonegaran is the residence of the second semi-independent Ruler at Solo, Pangeran Adipati Ario Mangkoonagoro, head of the dynasty of that name.

Though this princely residence is not so extensive as that of the Susuhunan of Solo, it is nevertheless of imposing proportions. When the visitor has passed the outer gateway, having driven for a long time beneath the high walls, the barracks of the private legions of the Prince are at his right and left beyond the front courtyard. A second gate gives on to the inner courtyard, across which is the entrance to the residence itself, surrounded by smaller buildings wherein the administrative offices are.

In front of the princely mansion, covering a great part of the courtyard, stands the audience hall, the largest pendoppo in Java. It has typical Javanese architectural form: an enormous roof sloping low to keep out the torrential tropical rains, and no walls, since these are superfluous in the unwavering heat of the climate. The marble floor is raised several steps above the level of the court, again as safe-guard against the deluge of the wet season; in the centre of the front is a wide porch where visitors alight from their vehicles and ascend the steps. At the back is the large annex like the front verandah of an ordinary house; it is called "Peringgitan", which means "the place where the shadow wayang is performed". Next to this is the large inner hall, with its great gala-bed, and beyond come the smaller living-rooms, the kitchens and the gardens.

In the large pendoppo, covering approximately fifteen hundred square yards, about six hundred guests are seated to witness the play about to be performed in the front of the hall where the actors will appear against a background of deep blue sky and the

GATUTKATJA (JAVANESE ACTOR) *(Water-colour)*

Performance in the Mangkoonegaran

silhouettes of palms. The courtyard is filled with hundreds upon hundreds of natives, for though the stage is a private amusement of the Javanese Ruler, he is so democratic, as we would term it, as to admit gladly any of his people who care to attend. Long before the beginning of the play the court is crowded with this popular audience sitting close together on their hassocks.

First they enjoy the spectacle of the arrival of the principal guests. The Oriental takes a great interest in his aristocracy, sharing this characteristic with his Occidental brother, if not outdoing him in zeal. He points out: this is the brother of the Sunan; those are his sons on the front row. Most of the native nobles appear in their native dress, their adornments glittering with jewels, their clasps and daggers in sheaths of gold.

Then the Europeans arrive, and though they be less gorgeously attired they also are a spectacle for the waiting crowds. Behind these again the hall fills with Javanese of social standing and their ladies. The dull yellow of the women's faces is pale above the peacock-blue, old-green and carmine silk of their jackets, and in their night-black hair the scented flowers gleam. When the Prince and his wife come and take their seats a small procession of courtiers follows; the orchestra plays softly; they move slowly, rhythmically as the barefooted Javanese always do, striding with unsurpassable dignity to their places.

Then the performance begins.

The orchestra has taken its place next to the gate from which the actors enter, and behind which they have their dressing-rooms. For it is the wayang-orang, the wayang played by men and women which we shall witness, a type of performance which originated from this very court, and was later imitated by other Rulers.

It is noteworthy that the wayang has created for itself forms of expression which touch every strata between two-dimensional decoration on the one extreme, and the fullest three-dimensional acting on the other. Javanese acting is, indeed, further advanced from the "picture surface" than our own, which is seen from one side only and produced therefore with but one side in mind. In Java the spectators sit on all four sides of the scene, so that their acting must be "in the round" as in the Greek theatre, and to a lesser degree in the Elizabethan.

An Artist in the Tropics

The wayang-beber is probably the oldest kind. It is a flat canvas on which purely decorative figures are painted, and which is unrolled and shown to the audience coincident with the progression of the story being read. The images on the white canvas appear simultaneously with the words they illustrate—a film with a considerable artistic difference.

The next form is the better-known shadow play. Here the mythological persons of ancient lore have been painted on buffalo leather, which has then been cut out and pierced. These silhouetted figures have an ornamental beauty so entirely Javanese that it has hardly yet been appreciated even by the cultured European, but can endure comparison as craft work and as pure design with our very highest products. The figures are coloured because they serve a double purpose, being seen from the one side as shadowed silhouettes on the screen, and from the other as coloured leather puppets. On this latter the manipulator sits, and the lamp which creates the shadows lights his stage. These wayang-koolit (koolit, meaning leather) are absolutely flat.

The third form of wayang is the semi-flat puppets with arms still made of buffalo leather, called "wayang-klitic". The fourth is that of the round puppets "wayang-golek", dressed with real linen or silk batik garments, and comparable with our marionettes. Here the form of the human figure is imitated, whereas hitherto it has been reduced to a convention almost abstract. The human body itself is recruited for the next stage, that of the "mask-play", called "wayang-topeng", and then it is a slight step to the eighteenth century in which the actor in person "took the stage".

The origin of the tales and stories performed by all these various wayang is the legends from the Indian Hindoo poetry such as the Mahabharata and Ramayana, but lore from the islands themselves affords many themes. In manuscripts of the eleventh century of our era these wayangs are referred to, and performances would have taken place even earlier.

The production which we witnessed was a revelation in that grandeur which, however much it is sought on the many-sided European stage, has far less place among its meaningless spectacularism than in the intrinsic greatness of the Javanese acting. This demands no theatrical scenery. Not even the Shakespearean notice is needed by which it was customary to make known that the scene was a seaport

"THE KING OF AWANGGA (JAVANESE ACTOR)"

Performance in the Mangkoonegaran

or a forest. But the Shakespearean device of textual reference is often used by the Javanese. We know how perfectly Shakespeare did it, conveying to his audience time or place of action, season and condition of weather.

> " Under the greenwood tree
> Who loves to lie with me
> And tune his merry note
> Unto the sweet bird's throat "

tells us at least as much as could trees of painted canvas realistically represented. So the Javanese speak of birds singing in the trees and the spectator knows that the scene is a forest. The European truly may be at a disadvantage here for he does not as a rule know a word of Javanese and thus misses the point, complaining of absence of scenery, of monotony, of obscurity, when actually the fault lies in himself.

One other interesting point of contact with Shakespearean drama was noticeable in this production which revealed itself particularly when the hero Angkawidyaya was taken by surprise by demons in a forest. His followers showed their kinship with the clowns of the Elizabethan stage, affording variety of subject matter as well as humorous relief. Alongside the main plot they work out another which not only affords relief to the audience but gives opportunity for rest to the actors in the main plot. Moreover, the contrast of the serious with the humorous, which so often in real life appears so unexpectedly, helps the playwright to increase the tension in the mind of the audience, and we think again of the knocking on the door in Macbeth or the churchyard scene in Hamlet.

Apart from these giants from the sub-plot, gods, demi-gods, demons and princes are the *dramatis personæ* of the wayang. The giants are generally recognisable by their fierce beards, enormous protruding teeth—often gilded—and wild gestures; noble characters have more refined and styleised faces, with more harmonious colouring in the costumes and a restraint of acting.

The foundation of most of the plays is, in essence, the conflict between good and evil. Notwithstanding the powerful giants, the devils, evil spirits and demons, at last the good triumphs, and so the wayang play has a spiritual significance which is manifested in the majestic, statuesque acting of the Orient. Rich attire is

91

An Artist in the Tropics

not disdained, but it is raised to a higher level by the potency of the play, and the regal taste of the Javanese courts. It is this inward significance which raises this art of Java so much above even such work as that of the Russian Ballets with their whirling, blinding colours scattered about with the same lack of restraint as the continual movement of their dancers, and suited primarily to the task of providing a dazzling spectacle to the thousands in our great cities who have spent the day in the dull slavery of our industrial lives which we hail as freedom. In spite of having reached the summit of technical skill, they show as possessing little more than amusement merit when compared with the synthesis of poetry, acting and colour expression which hold the Javanese stage.

There is a Biblical grandeur about the entrances of the princes with their counsellors, and their retinues. Solomon or Nebuchadnezzar must have walked with their courtiers thus, and thus appeared to their assembled vassals. And when Sin, personified in the tremendously powerful Bradjadenta, has been fought in vain by all earthly means, he at last is conquered by the holy godly weapon of the King of Awangga, and this climax of the play seems too the apotheosis of æsthetic and human emotions.

The entrance upon the scene of one of these groups of actors gives a sensation of sublimity which the Occident hardly knows. All fighting, all striding, all flight through the air is styleised, reduced to a fluent ornament of human gesture as we would compose a conventional ornament from the forms of a plant or blossom. In their merest walking one step is a complicated action: one leg is lifted sideways, one arm taking the silk shawl which hangs from the girdle and throwing it backwards, the other arm making a gesture in front of the body. The rhythmic movements are of an infinite grace and regal stateliness and nobility.

In this way the prince will enter, his followers alike, fluttering their silks, gleaming with gold of bracelets, of rings at their ankles, of the hilts of their swords, of elaborately worked and gilded leather helmets, and the golden beauty of their anointed bodies. They appear as gods and seem to float in the air; their faces are like masks, ornaments as each lovely figure is an ornament, styleised as each gesture is. The krisses are adorned with garlands of flowers, an adornment to which the Javanese give the poetical name of "the tassel which does not dread death".

Performance in the Mangkoonegaran

If the king speaks his attitude is the conventional one with the right arm outstretched in front of the body, rigid, commanding. The addressed listens with the head bowed, one arm folded in front of the breast humbly. It is as though Egyptian sculpture has come to life.

All obey the same rules of style, but this unity seems to add character to the persons and to make them more intense. The giants are quick, fierce and grim in their wild agitation, shaking their long hair and shaggy beards; they are like consuming flames of fire in the wind. Demons wear awe-inspiring livid masks, and are followed by Death himself.

Some of the actors are brothers of the Pangeran himself. They are blessed actors, but which, indeed, are not? Others may be gardeners, servants, officials, but none is a professional actor in our sense of the word, although they will rehearse almost every day.

Both the acting and the orchestra spoke a language new to us, but our royal host had had the order of the scenes and a résumé of the action written for us in our own language. Even without this, however, even had we been unable to follow exactly the plot, not been guided through this fairy garden, we would have realised the contact with eternity which sublime art of any kind, be it painting, acting, music, poetry or any other, always awakens. The hours sped. Deep in the blue night the dream of beauty came to an end. Long after we had taken our leave the enchantment lasted.

Chapter Twenty

Wayang Players

A CART heavily laden with instruments of the gamelan, that fascinating native orchestra with its drums, metallophones, its Arabian violin and flute; an unusual throng of men carrying parcels surrounding it; the strange little procession passes while we try to weary through that hour of despair in the still, hot afternoon which lies between the midday rest and the grateful coolness of evening. Custom assumes that we, as good Europeans, should be sitting clad in pyjamas in the porch of our room during this part of the day. We turn from our tea to the native boy who has stirred to take in the unusual pageant.

"What are these people going to do, Karto?" we ask.

He explains at length that they are the actors going to a Wayang performance at the hotel that evening. Almost unconsciously we prepare a sketchbook.

As soon as the sun has set, as the vague afterglow slowly fades from the grassfield, the first hesitatingly loose tones of the gamelan fall through the warm, still air like the first heavy raindrops of a tropical shower. In the hall of the hotel we find the chairs arranged along the walls, and a few guests are forgathered as a somewhat listless audience for the promised spectacle. Truly we must admit that the gamelan is not first rate; neither are the actors, but nevertheless the wayang carries with it the real grace of its origins, and gives beauty and style to the acting of these simple villagers. Once a coveted flower, a culture only of the courts of princes, the Wayang has now become a universal possession of the Javanese. Later, in the courts themselves, we were to hear these people's productions condemned as "kampong"—village stuff—but as we watch the opening movements of this exquisite drama interpreted in an age-old language of

A Warrior (Javanese Actor) *(Water-colour)*

Wayang Players

gesture, we cannot easily believe that there can be better. Even when we ourselves have enjoyed the rare privilege of witnessing a court production and so have some glimmering of standards of comparison, we incline to think that class feeling alloys the purity of artistic criticism in such condemnation, and remember the thrill of this first sight of the Wayang. We watch enthralled the two youths and the demon king who circles about them dancing, flame-like, ferocious, his silken garments floating about him during the fights. His demoniac restlessness serves to throw into relief the serenity of the youths and the exaltation as they suggest the flight through the air of the higher beings they are interpreting.

The friendly hotel manager answered our occasional questioning. "Where do these actors come from?" we have asked, and he has told us that they are the ordinary folk from the kampongs, but one or two of them have occasionally been given parts in the great performances arranged by Prince Paku Alam, "He that holds the Universe", as his name signifies, and head of one of the four remaining royal families of Java. Our informant indicated one of the youths. "A fine actor, don't you think?" he queried proudly. "Did you notice how beautifully he made his entrance on the scene?"

We agreed, wondering whether the star actors of the European theatre could have equalled this slim youth from a Javanese village in grace of movement; and our promptor, sensing sympathy and perhaps some degree of understanding, continued: "The majority of the guests of the hotel do not really care much for it. It is just that they feel it to be their duty as tourists to have seen it. Perhaps they are right; it is simple enough here. In the kratons and his eyes glowed with enthusiasm, "acting, costumes and music are much more refined, but the ordinary tourist is not allowed to be present at performances there. He is permitted to see the palace only on certain fixed days; the party is guided by officials; of the real court life he sees nothing. Perhaps," again he lapsed into pessimism born of long experience with the tribe tourist, "perhaps that, too, is best, for these court performances would prove somewhat overpowering to the casual visitor if he were tempted to stay. They go on for hours and hours, even for days, and few Europeans would have either the interest or the patience to sit it out."

He checked the diatribe to draw our attention to an old Javanese who was standing outside, and informed us that he was the manager

95

An Artist in the Tropics

of the company. We glanced up to see a weather-beaten face, the bones sticking through the skin.

"Many of the players are his children," our informant gossiped amiably, "and I believe that among those little ones who sit at the big guns and deal so lusty a blow when the occasion demands are some of his grandchildren who are being initiated into the company. In former years he used to act himself, but he has grown too old for that; now he is business manager, producer, *entrepreneur*, what you will. He it is who takes the money, and you may depend that he divides it among his troupe with no small amount of care and no lack of remembrance for his own share in the transaction."

For a moment the East seemed not so entirely remote from the West.

The drama ended, the dream music of the gamelan drifts away on a final quavering note; luring, questioning. We, with our curiosity for the players unsatisfied, follow them to the little passage which serves them as a dressing-room and where now they take off their fairy attire, their high head-coverings, their girdles, swords and arrows.

"Would one or two be willing to sit for a picture?" we ask the old man.

"Certainly. Does the Tuan desire to have them all at the same time for the Tuan's portrait? And," eagerly adds the business-managerial side of the old gentleman's mind, "how much is the Tuan going to pay?"

A little conference ensues, in which it is explained that the Tuan is not going to take a photograph, but means to make a picture in paint which will take very much longer. An agreement is made. The business-managerial mind still functions.

". . . If the Tuan will just give a small amount in advance, *satu perak* (one silver, as the Dutch Guilder has become to native Java), he may be sure they'll come to-morrow morning; quite sure, really, really they'll come in time."

He bows himself out, guilder in hand, and it happens accordingly. The next morning at the appointed hour the old man, whom we call "Pa" now with presumptuous familiarity, and his slender son are waiting—silently and movelessly sitting on the steps of our rooms. The smaller room wherein we have stored our trunks, will suit him admirably as a dressing-room, and the big porch is exalted to studio. Pa, in his capacity as stage-manager, assists the youth while he is

Wayang Players

dressing: he lets his eye dwell on him for a last fleeting moment to see if the bracelets are well adjusted and whether the silk shawls hanging from the girdle will hang and flutter well. Attired at last, and with his heavy make-up completed, the slender son appears; once he knows the attitude we prefer he places himself like a statue. On his hassocks, without a sound, the old man is shifting himself over the ground to get as near as possible. Squatting in his corner, his eyes following eagerly every movement and every line that is drawn on the canvas, he makes one think of a pet monkey, limbs folded, bright-eyed, intense, alert.

When we ask our fairy prince, during a short rest, what his name is, he murmurs shyly, "Sastrasentana"—a cascade of soft sounds—then father and son in turn whisper something about the lines and scratches on the canvas. And Pa demonstrates to the fairy prince how the Tuan does it: with this he makes his lines, a gesture explains; with that he blots out something, thus.

Again silence, and then the work continues. Sastrasentana now feels that he himself is part of the work; he holds his statue-attitude as though the world might perish did he make the slightest movement. To Pa the enchantment of the sketching is rivalled by the appeal of the apparatus one seems to need for it. There lies a stretcher; he solemnly examines its construction. That long case with three padlocks must be something of importance; who knows, maybe the Tuan will open it later. When that great moment really comes his eyes can hardly draw up the inventory of its contents quickly enough: rolls of canvas, wood for stretchers like that he has just examined, but bigger, bigger, cardboard boxes, a hammer. A small parcel of wedges tumbles to the floor temptingly close to his hand. He cannot resist and takes one out; what part does this play in all this Tuan magic? When in the next rest it is explained to him how they help to stretch the canvas he shakes his head at such ingenuity, but by this time his wandering curiosity has taken him to the canvas. He feels it appreciatively. How thick it is! "Banyak wang, banyak wang," he mutters, which is to say, "Much money, much money."

The fascination of wedges and canvas stretchers pales before that of the tubes of colour which emerge from the cardboard boxes, and of the yellow, golden and red paint which can be squeezed from them. He thinks it all marvellously well arranged, nods admiringly;

An Artist in the Tropics

yes, yes, beautifully arranged indeed. As organiser of his company he has a connoisseur's eye for such organisation.

He feels a new sense of importance at his own presence and assistance in all this curious business. Now and again the Tuan steps back from his work, moves the easel, takes oil from a bottle. The mistress does not speak nor help make the picture; she is writing all the time. It is splendid luck, he feels, to be here, and nobody from outside can see him, for the Tuan has had a curtain hung in the entrance of the porch at almost a man's height, and he sits guardedly behind it. Even when a pair of brown eyes, large and glittering, peer over the curtain's edge—a hotel boy wondering what this might be, a curtain, the Tuan and a Wayang Actor!—even then these eyes cannot see Pa in his observation corner.

Lunch time draws near.

"Shall we go on in the afternoon?"

Sastrasentana is quite prepared to do so; Pa acquiesces joyfully. "Must you not go and get something to eat?" We feel that even statues and princes must eat when they become incarnate in healthy Javanese youth. Pa, ever ready to cope with difficulties, will fetch some rice for him. So Sastrasentana has his lunch in the dressing-room, after which he lies down for a short nap; Pa asks, stooping, "Minta Permissie" to pass by, and joins his son. After a while he steals away soundlessly as the shadow of a mouse to get some rice.

Thus Sastrasentana comes several days.

There is nothing in the East Indies whereby one can tell that a certain day is the first of January; through the changeless seasons each day is like to each. Nothing, therefore, was to tell us, for we had not counted the days as we might have done since the manager of the Djocja Grand Hotel had presented his guests with a Dutch Christmas cake. Then one morning, when Sastrasentana has been busy in his dressing-room and appears ready for his part, he does not cross to the accustomed place, but, a little shyly, and fidgeting with his thin fingers at the silk gown, he comes straight to us. Very softly he begins to mutter in Malay. The Tuan, and the Mistress: we catch those words. And, "a happy journey back", and "free from sickness", and then, "Tahun baru" and we understand. "Tahun baru"—the new year. He is making an address on the

98

Wayang Players

occasion; and we, heavily, clumsily, self-consciously European . . . if only we had a word to say in return!

One other happening marks the New Year's Day. From the main building of the hotel a party emerges, boisterous, threatening our peace. Ready for the emergency we stop work, turn the canvas face to the wall, and wait for the storm to blow over. Sastrasentana, gauging the situation, has disappeared without a word to the refuge of his dressing-room. There he sits, quietly, imperturbably, majestic in spite of his simplicity, his body and soul unapproachable as though he were the Buddha. His legs are folded beneath his body and lie flat on the ground—the favourite attitude of the Oriental, the age-long attitude of meditation. Hardly moving his lips he says: "There will be Wayang again to-morrow." He has read the signs.

That day the whole hotel is in turmoil. Eighty-three Americans are coming; they are "doing" Java. Everywhere beds are being transported. Simon is quivering with hurry and importance—Simon, the satellite of Americans to an extent that neither Dutchman nor native pronounces his name save in nasal Manhattanese. Simon is here, Simon is there, and everywhere. He might be the Radjah of the hotel; in truth he is only an ordinary runner, but the lowliest runner has his day, and Simon is far from lowly. Is he not the backbone of the United States in the East Indies? He is Indian, not Malay, and looks terribly black and imposing with his heavy beard among the clean-shaven, yellowish Javanese. America in Java is Simon's domain. Neither Dutch nor other tourist wishes to be guided in the Simon-way, nor does he wish to guide them. "They are no good for me," he says with disdain, "but Americans!" and he pats his tourists on the back and grins with all his sharply-cut profile. He is the sheep dog driving the flock exactly where he desires it to go; telling it this, explaining it that, ordering everything and everybody. What Simon does is well done. Simon not on the spot, everyone feels helpless; no sooner does he return than he is in universal demand. "Ha, old chap . . ." the summons comes from every side.

Simon sticks up a notice in the hall; his orders. To-day: dinner at such and such an hour; Wayang performance. To-morrow: rise at 5.30; do the Borobudur Temple (the car will drive round it, don't bother to get out, commands Simon's edict; Simon will explain); then, departure by train to Bandoong, arrival about 6.0; dinner at

An Artist in the Tropics

9. Bandoong thus disposed of by implication in three crowded hours of glorious life before dinner, no time need be wasted on it the next morning. So, continues the order paper, rise at 5.30; breakfast at 6; automobiles for Batavia leave at 7; and so to the harbour, and away. Simon will see that everybody and everything gets safely on board; Simon will demonstrate to yet one more group from God's Own Country that Java can be seen in two days, for all its 50,800 square miles.

Just at the moment the Americans are feeling sleepy. Long, stiflingly hot train journeys have brought them from Batavia and Surabaya hither; little wonder they are weary. And a little bored perhaps, for nothing exciting happened. Ordinary trains, a railroad, no wildernesses of desolating wildness, no herds of elephants blocking the road, no tigers. A few chickens were the only earnest of the zoology of the island and provided no emotions. So are they sleepy. But Simon says: first we'll have wayang, you get your dinner after that, then you may go to bed. Simon's word is law, and the Americans sit and wait, their appearance amazingly combining the alert efficiency of so many aeroplanes and the dull acceptancy of a Victorian ladies' working party. They are to have half-an-hour's dose of the arts of Java as an apéritif for dinner. But Simon neither sits nor waits. He drives the Javanese at American pace. "Not so much chatter," he commands from his self-elected post as stage manager. "We'll have some fighting, but don't wait too long in starting it." They like the fighting, he grins to us in an aside as we watch actors and audience from our own coign of vantage, but he observes the Americans rubbing sleepy eyes, and with a born instinct for the whims of his public, hastens the last and quite meaningless pageant across the stage, quickens the music, and "That is enough, clear away all of you." Simon has presented the Wayang. "The Anklung," he announces, "rural Javanese music." The native bamboo instrument is displayed and even played upon for nearly three minutes. Away with it. Shadow performance now. What, is this lamp not going to burn well? Simon will look at it. "There you are, you silly fellows; that's fixed it, eh?" Java stands a little out of countenance, a little ashamed, as Simon bridges the gulf between East and West; America applauds. They have seen the soul of Java. "Time for dinner now," says Simon; and America, replete with artistic sensation, cheers up.

Wayang Players

The next morning, before the eighty-three are to be sent to the train, Pa comes by, followed by two others carrying stage-stuff in parcels. After a few minutes they return.

"That was anything but fine, last night," we say.

Shyness and silence among the three. We remember those parcels and suspect something. "What have you done with your things? I thought I saw you carrying them just now?"

"A Tuan America wanted to buy," admits Pa.

"You sold?"

"Yes."

"But won't you need your properties yourselves?"

Pa grins. He shuffles nearer on his hassocks lest Javanese walls have American ears, and confides: "Some old stuff, no use for our work any more."

We smile understandingly, and Pa, able to restrain himself no longer, whispers the price he has managed to get, grinning over his success. Pa has haunted our porch to tender us this pleasant confidence, and now they disappear.

When, after a time, a wayang performance again takes place, Java is obviously avenged for that disquieting American evening. As they pass us on their way home, Pa says good-night with a meaningful smile. Out into the Javanese night his happy company carry their beautiful new properties.

Chapter Twenty One

Poodyon

"Poodyon, Hotel Justina" (three times underlined). "Delightful. Stay there." So we were admonished in the list of hotels and addresses with which friends had supplied us before we left Europe. To the traveller who has endured the suffocating heat and choking volcanic dust of Mid-Java it is a marvellous refreshment to wander about in the invigorating mountain air of Poodyon.

Every walk, and there are many, is a delight. One takes us to a roaring waterfall, reached after following a path which yields a tremendous view over the wide plain of Malang. Sloping paths lead to villages, bright mountain brooklets where buffaloes bathe, women do their washing, or youngsters fill bamboo tubes as large as themselves with fresh water, border them.

Above, from the hotel gardens, one sees the wide mountain lands on the far side of the deep valley. Away to the left Mount Kawi slopes down in the distance, and treacherous volcanic Mount Kloot lifts its notched silhouette, wild and broken. To the right the Dorowati lies. The sun will set behind its highest peak. Facing it Mount Weliran smokes, with its heavy sulphur fumes pale and strange against the darkening skies, the last light of the sun still held on its mighty summit when the slopes of the valley where we stand are already enveloped in shadow. On the dark breasts of the mountains the evening fires of the watchhouses sparkle like half-hidden jewels.

Marigolds, roses and convolvuluses bloom in the garden on the cool mountain slope, together with violets and forget-me-nots. Lower down in the nursery beds, artichokes, strawberries and many other fruits and vegetables thrive.

Round us floats the healing quietude of the countryside, deeper and deeper falls the silence as the evening grows darker. A solitary ox-cart crunches slowly over the gravel of the road . . . and nothing further stirs.

TERRASSED RICEFIELDS, POODYON (*Drawing*)

Chapter Twenty Two

Tosari and Mount Bromo

TOSARI is the chief health resort of East Java, and its own foremost sight is Mount Bromo, the mightiest of Java's volcanoes. What delight it is to leave behind the hot town of Pasoorooan and breathe the cooler mountain air, even though we have been the guests of the Resident there and in his palatial house have lived as coolly and comfortably as the terrific heat permitted.

Pasoorooan itself is not very important. It is old-fashioned, and the Residential House also is, which means that it is of almost formidable dimensions, with wide front verandah, spacious central corridor dividing the house in two and having rooms on either side, and a back verandah with a wide terrace overlooking the garden. This is the typical arrangement for a house in the East Indies. A wide lawn lies between the house and the main road; it has beautiful trees, and in a pond the Victoria lily blooms.

We have visited the ancient Hindoo Bath, Banjoo Biroo, the Blue Water. It is a great pond enclosed by thick foliage, and the water of the well is strangely blue as legend has it that it has been for ages. Old Hindoo sculpture has been found here, and has been put up again with reverence. Hundreds of monkeys inhabit the surrounding trees, and come down in dozens in friendly intercourse with the visitors to the place.

We pass on along an ever winding road up the steep slope, and gradually the landscape beneath us spreads wider and wider. The slopes are covered with the only needle-leaved trees of the East, the "tjemaras" which give quite an Occidental character to the scenery.

On the top of the high hills Tosari lies. Mists and clouds often drift over it, but now and again they are dispersed by the sun and the distant landscape is unveiled. The old inhabitants of the lonely

An Artist in the Tropics

mountain tops have adhered to the Hindoo religion, although many centuries since Mohammedanism held sway everywhere else. Wonokriti, Serdaeng and Proowono are their villages; bare, poor, humble rows of huts, they have no longer anything to attract us, but the stranger always visits them and is duly pestered by groups of children begging coppers. The white man is to their population what the English tourist is in Volendam, an object of legitimate plunder. All the time the children bother you with their "minta presen, minta presen"[1], or insist on showing you the way which clearly manifests itself, in spite of all you may say or shout at them.

Around lie the brown fields, the undulating lands where vegetables are grown, divided by the thin tjemara trees.

But the wild Bromo eclipses altogether this softer landscape. One goes there at night, riding by moonlight on horseback. Hour after hour passes unbroken save by the gusts of the wind through the tjemara trees, until at last we reach the Moongal Pass, and suddenly can look down into the low sea of blackish sand—the Bromo Sand Sea. Black it is as if one had arrived in some subterranean world; a landscape of hell. Everything is dead; everything is black. Down in the depths the winds have streaked a design in the restless sand; it looks as if the heart of the world had bled and coagulated on the day of creation.

As if neither plant nor animal had ever lived on earth, so devoid of life lies this wide pit of horror, empty, lonely, incredibly barren. The wind rushes across it, drives the ashy powder upward in frenzy, and then it slowly is drawn back again. Thus it has been caught up, thus abandoned, through century after vain century.

Before us, across the tortured sea, an unwieldy cone rises, with sides carved. It is Mount Batok, black also. Beyond it stream the unceasing vapours of the poisonous Bromo crater. Both are children of this enormous pit into which one gazes. When the traveller has climbed down the steep slope into the sand sea, where vegetation halts, his horse soon brings him round the Batok's cone. Then slowly the flat sands begin to slope, the ground to change into rough ashes and cinder stone cracking beneath the hoofs of the horse. Higher and higher yet; the waves of lava have congealed as they have flowed down from the crater. It seems a stormy sea gone solid, with waves become stone when they have lost their power

---

[1] "Minta presen": "Give me a present," i.e. money.

CRATER OF MOUNT BROMO *(Drawing)*

Tosari and Mount Bromo

to combat the deadening cold which seized them in their course, their energy too far spent to escape.

Higher and higher still the horse climbs. Then it stays behind while the traveller ascends yet farther. Wider and wider the wild sea beneath becomes, just as the landscape opened out beneath us on the road to Tosari. Thick clouds of smoke are blown to tatters in the air, the winds strengthen as we rise. Then abruptly the solid earth ends, falls away before our feet; it is the immense crater, an inverted cone with carved walls sloping down, and in its depth thick skeins of vapour twist and roll from beneath the lumps and clods of the sulphurous, steaming bottom. The heavy silence of eternal death is around us.

Chapter Twenty Three

Barang Lama

"HONESTLY, honestly barang lama.[1] Genuine old things, lama betool ini.[2] It is from Bangkalan in Madura; very, very old, Modyopahit[3]. The tuan can have it very cheap. Honestly nommer satoe.[4] Yes, bagoos, bagoos."[5]

Thus the Madurese tradesman recommends his wares. He has discovered our interest in old handwoven materials, has brought along a half dozen of his fraternity, and they swear that everything they proffer is valuable and antique.

Every kind of rubbish they have brought to-day. There is a rack such as is used for hanging over the material to be batikked —the upper part beautifully carved, but the rest a poorly made modern addition. Sets for sirih;[6] plates in brass or earthenware; old scripts on the leaves of the lontar palm, which are pierced at the ends and tied together; silver boxes—"nicely carved this one, bagoos, bagoos";[5] a kriss brought forth from a big canvas bag with no end of bric-a-brac.

"Real silver," he says, and knocks on the sheath of a dagger; and then with a desperate pull, with teeth glittering and eyes wide with agitation, his long hair blown over his face from beneath his loosely flapping headgear, he snatches the weapon from its sheath like a pirate about to take our lives. His comrades unpack their loads with equal zeal. Some are as wild-looking as he, others are quietly sly behind the unmoving masks of their faces.

One with a sirih-stand (a bowl with a tray whereon stand several tiny brass or silver pots) on his head approaches poising his burden, sinks silently down on his hassocks mysteriously, and elects to remain

[1] Antiques.
[2] It's really old.
[3] A Javanese kingdom from circa 1300–1500.
[4] First rate.
[5] Fine.
[6] A vegetable preparation for chewing.

Mount Merapi (*Etching*)

Barang Lama

silent and motionless as an image till those who came first have had their opportunity. Soon we are completely surrounded by a medley of cow-bells, cigarette cases, metalwork of all kinds brilliantly scrubbed and polished.

The least vague sign of interest in any object sets up a shrill chorus of "Berapa, berapa, berapa?[1] What will the tuan give? The tuan may bargain, boleh tawar.[2] Truly the tuan may. How much will he give?"

And when, after long conversations among themselves, with much shaking of heads and pointing with their thumbs in the Javanese fashion, the whole throng have packed their belongings and disappeared, the gentleman of the kriss returns and, with an attitude worthy of Columbus with his egg, shows us not only *one* kriss but triumphantly waves *two* in the air and remarks convincingly:

"Sir, if you are not going to have one kriss, why not take these two together? Lama betool. You can have them for a song. Have a pair of them."

Nevertheless we do not add one kriss even to the growing burden of our luggage.

[1]How much.   [2]Make an offer.

Chapter Twenty Four

Madura Island

A TINY launch, such as would serve no more dignified purpose in
a European port than that of bringing one from the ship to the
wharf, runs from Java's commercial town, Surabaya, to Madura
Island, and puts you off at a hamlet.

With all our luggage we are marooned on the shore. A throng
of wildly gesticulating, shouting, fierce-looking fellows seize an
easel, a trunk or two, or whatever else they can get a hold of, and
lead the way into the gathering dusk with their trophies, like brigands
after a raid. Across the rails of the steam-tram they bring us to the
point where the main road begins, then they plant down our belongings and, with the least circumlocution, demand pay for their services.
Whereupon they sit down upon their hassocks, their arms spread out
straight across their knees, and wait to see what will happen next.
For no tram goes any more to-day since it is already late afternoon,
and as travellers are scarce here they are naturally intrigued as to
what the white people will do other than stand helplessly next their
trunks and face the fact that there is nothing to carry them anywhere. For the "blandas" it is also a problem. It will soon be
dark, dusk is short in the tropics, and every minute the sun sinks
lower and lower.

From Surabaya we had wired for an automobile, and received
an affirmative reply, but no car has materialised. Nothing else
suggests itself than to try to telephone to the nearest place for another,
but a conversation on the telephone is a difficult achievement when
the blanda hardly knows Malay and a Chinaman at the other end
speaks it with a Chinese pronunciation which is practically incomprehensible to any newcomer in the East. The conversation somehow brought to an end, there is nothing to be done other than resume

AT KALIANGET, MADURA (Drawing)

Madura Island

our vigil and hope that the promised car will come this time. It should come from the not too distant Bangkalan, and will have to take us to Pamekasan, half way down the island. We wait and wait; more and more stage pirates gather round us, and two offer a diversion by killing a hen. Then again we peer and strain our sight along the darkening road.

After what seems an eternity a car does arrive. With the fresh blood of their slaughtered hen on their hands, the bronzed Madurese fishermen hoist our trunks into it and away we go as we have gone so many times of late towards the unknown by car, by boat, by train or carriage. On the sea, which the road skirts, white, light fishing proas[1] float on the deep blue; and at our left the hilly land catches here and there the last light of the sun. We dash on, and every time we pass a house, a hamlet, or a group of the rough natives, a wild shouting demonstrates their interest in the unheard-of phenomenon of white folk arriving by night on the island.

The next day we are brought on from Pamekasan to the east of the island, where at Kalianget the salt pans are—a valuable State monopoly. The coast is flat, the bay is wide, and beyond it rise the enormous mountains of East Java. Silent women with baskets poised on their heads stride by in the dusk. The land is flat, like the meadows of Holland, and an occasional drawbridge emphasises the illusion. Here and there a native scoops the water into the salt pans with a basket on a stick. Quickly the water will evaporate in the tropical heat of the morrow and soon layers of salt will cover the ground. This is gathered into sheds and pressed into blocks. There is a huge hall where the machines stand, a store-room with everything carefully labelled—everything clean and scientific as a chemist's shop.

All along the coast the fragile proas lie like marine creatures cast up by the sea. The Madurese loves to adorn his vessel with fine woodcarving and bright colouring: black alternates with pure white and fierce vermilion, blue and lacquer green. Stern beyond carved stern lifts itself steeply from the bodies of the vessels, looking like some exquisite sequence of ornaments designed upon the motive of the tossing waves themselves.

The northern shore, with its golden sands, also reminds one of Holland, but neither the villages nor the typically oriental fishermen

[1]Boats.

An Artist in the Tropics

have any affinity with the West. Little villages such as Marengan, Amboonten, or Sloppeng have the charm of the picturesque carelessness and filthiness characteristic of the East: a gaily coloured market, a fine shore, narrow streets with shops and stands. On the hilly ground the cacti grow and cattle are reared. The cow is the chief pride of many a Madurese. Once a year great festivals are held and races arranged wherein the bulls, garlanded with flowers, take part. For those brief hours the great god Pan, dear god of country life, governs the Madurese world.

Fishing-Boats on the Shore (Drawing)

Chapter Twenty Five

Concert Giving

"So you are the people who have come for the concert to-morrow?" Thus are we greeted somewhere. "Well, it is nice to have a chat with somebody newly arrived from Holland about the stuff they call 'art' there now-a-days. Perhaps you can enlighten us as to what they are driving at over there. Is that modern stuff really looked at or taken seriously?"

"?"

"Yes, Madame, what will be the end of it, I ask you? I adore music, but when I have been in business all day long I really cannot be bothered with compositions which no man on earth could understand. Then I'm told: you should listen, you should try to follow. Now, do you think there is anything in it to follow, any thought at all? Some of that boring stuff of Beethoven, for example. What do you think?"

We dare to assume that Beethoven added sense to sound, and hastily change the subject to literature to avoid the pitfalls of the sister art since discussion is unlikely to get us further. But our interrogator is not easily put off.

"You may be right, but, whether it be literature or music, it should say something to the plain man surely. What use is it otherwise? Take a novel by Walter Scott for instance. There is history in it, and that is something worthy. Better than these descriptions of back streets in the East End with all their filth and vulgarity which seem to be the literary fashion now. The man who writes this sordid stuff they call the big man now, don't they? I ask you: must we all take to the slums or should we try to keep out of them? I can't understand these so-called authors. And the immorality they spread!"

An Artist in the Tropics

We make an effort to defend all art, even that outside the historic. "But what, my dear sir, can they have for a subject better than a fine story which really happened? Surely that is better than all this fanciful nonsense. Well, you at any rate are lucky: it must be jolly to go about where you like and paint what you like. Painting must be a pleasant sort of sport."

"Sport," we meditate perplexedly, but our host is already expanding. "Rather difficult though to catch the native type exactly. One doesn't often see it done. Do you know that poster for William III cigars? No? A gentleman is having a cigar offered him by his boy, his djongos.[1] It isn't quite the native as we get to know him but it's getting near the type. Have you tried painting the natives?"

Every reception is a fresh surprise, and if Philistine causerie upon art is among the most difficult there are compensations. In large or small places one cannot guess what people will be encountered or what their manners will be. When we had to pay our first visit to a private house we happened to have some difficulty in finding the place. Entering the gate we saw only white pillars on which the roof rested, the spaces between being closed by matting sunblinds. No bell; no knocker. We did not yet know that it was *de rigueur* to shout, and hesitated to do anything so demonstrative in front of this dignified mansion. We explored the flanks of the house and found some native servants, who beckoned us to follow to the back and then indicated that we should follow up the back verandah. To our European minds this seemed a little too presumptuous, and we sent in a note on our card. Later we heard how shocked our hostess had been at our incivility in omitting to shout.

At another place perhaps a musician is received by amateur colleagues who have a branch establishment of Debussy. They rapidly make it clear to you that they hold the monopoly of modern music and appreciation in the East.

To the professional musician a great trouble is that no European instrument can stand the moisture, the heat, and the insects for very long. Soon the keys of a piano will not move any more; tuners are *rara avis* and expensive because of the enormous distances they must travel to effect their work. Moreover, it is a good old custom that the club-house pianos, being used for dance music

[1] Native servant.

112

Concert Giving

on many evenings and having produced tunes for hours, are given a drink also, and to this end a glass of champagne or beer is poured into the instrument. In Surabaya we found that a brand new concert grand had evidently been treated that way already although the building where it stood was not yet finished. In the club-house at Batavia we found them better prepared for these festive eventualities. Not only do they keep the piano locked, but since that would be insufficient, a couple of strong iron bolts secure a long iron rod which prevents the piano being opened. A formidable padlock provides the ultimate security.

"Otherwise," remarked the secretary significantly, "the piano would suffer too much from the dampness."

Apart from three or four of the larger towns, the club-house in the East Indies is the only public building available for whatever entertainment is toward. That means that in the adjoining room the rhythmic click of billiard balls provides an accompaniment to the violinist, for why should anyone stop the noble game of billiards for some scraping on a violin? What would become of freedom if any such stoppage were imposed, and anyway do not these members of the club pay their subscriptions?

In such remote places as Europe it is customary for the platform to be reserved for the artistes. So many countries, so many customs! Here it is the domain of numerous flapping and fluttering bats, which the musicians disturb from rest; and as soon as the lamps are lighted other visitors come: mosquitoes, flies, buzzing beetles. Also the dogs like it, although their oversensitive ears often cause them to add their quota to the performance. On these occasions the worst sinners will be summarily ejected, but it is not easy to keep them out of an oriental building open and accessible from all sides. From the environs the penetrating chirping of millions of crickets joins in.

The menagerie of the tropics also provides other candidates for stage honours. Tyityaks, the small wall-lizards, scarcely count, but the big ones, tokkehs, can make a respectable noise at awkward moments. The keys of the piano, when not entirely immovable, generally rouse clouds of moths and mosquitoes, the latter demanding blood for their broken peace. It may also happen that the instrument is the lawful domicile of a nest of ants, tiny ones, it is true, which do not bite very much, but their perambulation across one's fingers tends to interfere with the rendering of the accompaniment.

An Artist in the Tropics

A pianist at first may be disappointed to discover that many of the keys of his instrument will not move, but later he learns that this may have advantages. We were amazed to hear that some Russian pianist had complained twice in one town on the subject. Of course, he was informed the committee knew of the matter, for he had said all that once before. These exacting musicians!

Of acoustics one is not so concerned with the sounds in the halls quite so much as with those which come from without, for if there be walls these are so replete with the very necessary ventilation grates that one hears these extraneous noises excellently. So we heard another pianist play a Beethoven sonata to the accompaniment of a lemonade seller's bell, a novel and interesting combination embellished by the grinding of passing tramway cars. The musician was what is considered a great pianist out there; at least his hands were photographed and exhibited at the booking office, so that want of respect for those was not the reason of the lemonade vendor's activity.

The primary reason for attending a concert is generally that it is being followed by a dance. Thus it happens that when we are inspecting the hall early in the day and inquire whether we had better begin at the announced time or give our audience some minutes' grace we are asked to be exact.

"They know there is a dance when your concert is through, and as they will be wanting to dance the sooner it is over the better."

This naïve reminder of our place in the scheme of things was given at Solo, one of the "big" places. It is better to draw a veil over many smaller ones.

Occasionally it has been tried with little success to drill natives to play European notes, and then a remarkable second concert follows the first. Elsewhere youths who play the banjo are plentiful, but if these do not exist the dance music cannot be omitted, and the visiting musicians are requested to play some dances. Strangely enough they sometimes do not accede joyfully to this demand. But there is a way out: somebody dashes home in a car and fetches the musician's substitute—the uncomplaining gramophone.

In the good old days these festivities achieved heights: billiard balls were sent hurtling through clocks or a bonfire made of the club-house furniture. But alas, the days of great deeds are over, and there is no such vital reaction to Beethoven.

SWEETMEAT SELLERS *(Drawing)*

Concert Giving

When a concert is over it may prove as difficult to depart as it proved to arrive, for a chat is deemed indispensable. As for arriving it were best illustrated by an example.

The traveller who studies the steam tram guide finds that he is to arrive at Perlak at 2 o'clock if he leaves Medan at 6 a.m. That, it is true, means early rising, for bags and baggage have to be taken; it also seems rather long for travel, but one is consoled by the thought that we shall be at our destination by 2 o'clock and can get a rest in the afternoon and be fresh for the concert in the evening. The tram wagons prove to be very small, very close, very dirty, slow and bumping, but they persevere and actually arrive at their station at 2 o'clock. A member of the committee meets us. He says: "Just a few minutes' walk and there, you see. . . ."

The hall, we surmise.

"The boat," he says.

Away we go. For two hours more we travel steadily up the incredibly monotonous river only surpassed by the incredibly monotonous lands with which the tram has acquainted us. Thick vegetation is on either side. One crocodile we discover, but it shows no sign of interest in us. At last, the landing stage appears.

"I kept a lorry waiting," says our guide cheerfully.

Gone is the hope of afternoon rest. We meditate which of us is the more miserable, but neither have the courage to start an inquiry on the matter. We climb the lorry, which consists of a few primitive seats on a wooden floor with four wheels. Four Chinamen are waiting to push us on, and when we and our luggage are stowed aboard they drive off with us into the virgin woods. We are beyond counting time by now, but it probably lasted about an hour and a half. A sudden shouting of the Chinese stirs us from our listlessness. The coolies hold back as much as possible; a similar vehicle appears from the opposite direction filled with oil-pipes. There is no need to argue which is the heavier trolley. We alight, and the coolies simply put our carriage alongside the road until the other has passed. Then we return and recommence our switchback ride. At last our destination is reached.

We are brought to the club, and when the concert is over—the appreciation of the audience has made up for many discomforts—we hear that the financial results have succeeded beyond expectations,

An Artist in the Tropics

and they round off upwards the agreed fee. That is not a musician's daily lot!

The other extreme of this experience is when we arrive, when and where according to all precedent we cannot. A telegram beforehand is of no avail. If it is customary to take three days in covering a certain distance why should a telegram, a specially chartered car which takes a short cut and does the journey in twelve hours, be taken into account? We learn next day that our telegram did arrive, but that no attention was paid to it because everybody took three days to do the trip. We did not trouble to explain that we wanted to catch a boat which calls once a week only, and thus to save six days.

In small places the comfort which the halls lack is often made up for by helpfulness. It may happen that the harbourmaster lends the lamps of the port to provide footlights. When, after an interval, the performers reappear on the platform, the powerful lights have gone. "What has happened to our footlights?" they query the audience, and at once a voice from the multitude replies: "Fetched away. The port must be lighted. A ship is coming in." We bow to the inevitable, our gratitude to the harbourmaster no less for half a concert loan of footlights, than it would have been for complete service. Neither musicians nor audience were disappointed at their disappearance and all remained in high spirits.

The artists' rooms as a rule are beyond description. In most cases nobody takes any care of them, and so one finds a musty corner dimly lit by a smoking lamp, a rickety chair, a dirty table, and no more. Being hardly ever used by human beings, it is the haunt of rats, mice and cockroaches, whilst bats hang in the corners of the ceiling in undisturbed rest.

This neglect may not be calculated to provide the right atmosphere for an artist's work, but occasionally one cannot complain about the room since it does not exist, but a back corner of the stage performs the purpose. On the other hand, occasionally everything is spick and span, people have troubled to bring chairs, a washstand and other things from their homes. Once, in a far-off place, a lady had managed to give the otherwise gruesome dressing-room the appearance of a boudoir, and the water in the jug was scented with the little flowers which the natives like as a perfume—it seemed to be in readiness for an oriental princess.

Concert Giving

The conditions of the artists' room can be taken as an indication of the character of the audience. It may be that among them is a group more prone to pay homage to Bacchus than to the Muses, and then it may mean a keen tussle between these and their more æsthetic neighbours.

Also it happens that an audience has forgathered by car from their estates, of people who will not miss any chance of contact with the arts, and then one has the keenest audience in the world, and to the performers, as to themselves, the evening is one of real refreshment. "Every audience gets its own value" a colleague once rightly said.

When at the end, towards midnight—for concerts do not start until nine—a circle is formed, the champagne corks begin to pop. The hospitable intention is admirable, but sometimes it means rather a strain for worn-out travellers who have been going about since six in the morning, hurrying and travelling without ceasing in the heat: riding, driving, sailing, packing and unpacking, changing dress for the journey, changing dress for the concert, and moving all the time. Generally an hour or so is considered to be enough for this social function, and many in the circle nod kindly and understandingly when we explain that the time has come for us to rest and take hearty farewell.

In the regions where Bacchus is honoured, however, your audience has different expectations from artists. The travelling-fare earner, as the musician is popularly assumed to be by such a group, is equally assumed to be most amusing after the official programme is over.

"Sometimes," we were once informed, "these artists are a deception. This man So-and-So, for instance, is a good enough actor and is, I am told, very much appreciated in Holland, but do you think the fellow could tell one single anecdote after the play?"

We bowed before the criterion. We felt quite certainly that upon us too this damning judgment fell, but it was impossible to save the situation and we left it to the band to play "Yes, we have no Bananas" and "Valencia" with no assistance to the party from us as *raconteurs*.

Escaped after such an evening's work, not even a towering palm or stately waringin tree etched marvellously against the silver-blue moonlit sky can hold our attention. We dully dream through a

An Artist in the Tropics

heavy but unrefreshing sleep. Subconsciously our tired minds are registering the warning: presently you must get up again. Now and again one gets out of bed to fetch the sticky oil lamp and search for a mosquito which has percolated one of the many holes of the mosquito net. The marauder discovered, he is attacked vigorously with the bunch of leaf-ribs tied together which is to hand at every Javanese bed-side for this very purpose, and whether the campaign has been crowned with success or not one tries to sleep again.

With the aid of the aforementioned oil lamp you often have to get up in Java at five or half-past four, in the thick darkness, to catch the train at six o'clock. The hotel boy is bidden to knock you up at "stenga lima"—half-past four—and this stenga lima has remained with us as a nightmare wherein the victim sees himself, sleepily nid-nodding in the hotel omnibus, bumping over the rough streets of a deserted town in the dead silence of the night.

For such adventures an occasional stay with a friendly family is recompense. We once had a host whose care went so far as to warn us against having the window open at night for fear of catching cold—an unheeded warning in a place as broiling as Batavia. In a fashionable hotel it may happen that first a jazz band and later a private saxophone amateur makes music through the still watches of the night, and in the sleepless tropic night that instrument can utter such unearthly shrieks as no European ear other than its master's can endure. Even for a musician this orchestral aftermath to the efforts of an ordinary band and a Hawai-band playing together during dinner proves to be "that little more and how much it was". And the poor traveller, who has seen forests, fields and plains whirl by his train window all through the day, has endless couples whirling past his plate during this too-musical dinner.

Outside Java itself, where the principal routes at least are covered by the railways, trains are only found on one or two stretches in Sumatra. In all the other islands of the archipelago the motor-car is the only means of transit, and that as far as roads have been constructed in its wild and partly inaccessible mountains and marshes. Some of the cars are not first-class. To race in a defective machine along an unknown road in the dark night, swaying to left and right, then suddenly to halt with a jerk, go on with another, till at last the vehicle sticks in a ditch alongside the road, is far from amusing, especially as the ditch does not spell the end of the adventure, for one

DANCING GIRL, BALI *(Etching)*

Concert Giving

has to manage somehow to get forward or back with all one's impedimenta with the aid of another car obtained from miles and miles away. A concert had to be given up more than once, the audience losing patience and going home.

In the old days, when visitors from Europe were rare, hospitality was great. Even now it may be counted among the assured delights of a visit. We had only been in Java for a week or so when a telephone message informed us that in the next town we were visiting a whole house would be placed at our disposal, together with the native servants. So we took possession, and our few words of Malay were completed by gesticulations from which the boy and the cook deduced our needs. It subsequently transpired that we had only upset them once by getting up at eight o'clock, which seemed to us a reasonable hour for rising since we had given a concert the evening before, but "pookool delapan"—eight o'clock—the boy had repeated in disgust all the next day. For the native servant is as regular as clockwork, an extraordinary phenomenon since time does not exist to him. A pleasant thought, we meditate, not to know how old one is, nor to care, but only to be concerned with time in its relation to other people's getting up at eight instead of six.

When, too soon for our liking, an end has come to this pleasant stay, the boy is punctual to see that at "stenga lima" we are off with bag and baggage, and we go on our way rejoicing with a basket of excellent fruit and a load of poetical blessings.

Thus the travelling musician's life is a continuous change of good and bad luck, as their progress is a continuous change of good and bad club-houses. The names of these prove that poetry does not stop with the natives, for have we not performed at "The Harmony", "Concordia", "The Wet Mine", "Mud Delight"—incredible name —or "Our Pleasure". The very names should make us feel at home. Despite their suggestion of harmony, however, there were occasions when we found ourselves embroiled in the strife of rival factions, and if one party came into the club-house, the other would vacate the building. Ill or well, good or bad, easy or difficult, a concert tour through the East Indies may be relied upon to bring experience and to establish contact with strange and delightful human souls.

Chapter Twenty Six

To Bali

BALI!

Had somebody said to us some time ago: "To-morrow we go to Bali", we should almost have jumped with delight. For Bali is famous; we knew it from descriptions, from photographs, from repute of its glorious handwoven materials, its temples, its feasts, the burning of the dead, its whole gamut of unspoilt native culture, as well as for the unsurpassed hydraulic engineering which, constructed partly underground, partly above, irrigates the rice-fields.

Why then have we lost the desire to visit a place so teeming with interest? Because we have just discovered in a newspaper a huge announcement, ornamented with black index hands from right and left, and headed "Burning of the Dead". Thus:

 BURNING OF THE DEAD

Have you ever seen this ritual Buddist Ceremony (in connection with the Popular Festivals)?????

COME WITH US TO BALI!!

Motor-car trips. Swimming. Rowing. Dancing. Riding. Visits to Temples and Museums. Lawn Tennis. Football, etc., etc.

UNDER THE MANAGEMENT OF A THOROUGHLY RELIABLE COURIER

The five question marks are a faithful transcription of this broad invitation, and we wonder whether these or the enumeration

"A STREET SCENE, BALI"

To Bali

of delights will prove the more attractive. It is not easy to conjecture why anybody should go to Bali for the purpose of making automobile trips, of swimming, rowing, dancing, or riding on horseback, since any of these joys are available anywhere else without the expense of travel to so far a place. But evidently the trip to Bali is "done" by the "best people" lured by the advertisements, as we discover when on board the boat all first-class accommodation has been monopolised by the thoroughly reliable courier, and we find ourselves relegated to a primitive second-class cabin, at the price of a first-class ticket which allows us the honour of sharing meals with the first-class dancers and equestrians.

The advertisement responders arrive. They are mostly Chinese disguised as Europeans—the plutocracy of the Land of the Dragon. As soon as they are on board the ladies change their uncomfortable high-heeled shoes and their stockings for the customary bare feet, for " new garments cleave not to their mould but with the aid of use ". Eau-de-Cologne is produced from all bags; opera glasses, kodaks, hand baskets and blue spectacles follow.

There is much ado about baggage, the inevitable fussing of people not accustomed to travel. Only one bag is left on deck. An attaché case? No, a camouflaged gramophone, which, in the delight of novelty, gets itself wound up the wrong way, but seems undisturbed by this cavalier treatment, and soon begins with the nasal intonation of its kind to wheeze out the silly dance music which automatically pursues us all over the East. The hand-bags, thermos flasks and cake tins are opened to provide more substantial fare. Hardboiled eggs are chipped by heavily-ringed fingers; gold and jewels glitter everywhere.

Thus we go out to Bali.

Hardly has our steamer arrived at the port of the village Singaradja when proas in enormous quantities rush to meet us and bring us ashore. Together with an American lady and gentleman, who are "doing" some forty countries, we have agreed to share a punt and to deal with the problem of finding accommodation. It is late in the afternoon, Bali is not likely to provide room for such an influx of visitors, and the thoroughly reliable courier will doubtless have done his work as efficiently as he had on the boat. So we may have to go on to another town. By signalling we have made sure of one of the proas. When our luggage is brought down by a lively Balinese,

An Artist in the Tropics

we find a youth already in possession of our proa, and just as we push off another jumps in. To any who know the East it is unnecessary to report that these were the inevitable half-castes with their mandolins.

At the shore there is a great tumult of passengers, trunks, and carriers. First the ladies are brought to land safely. In the meantime our own unbidden guests have disappeared, leaving anyone who will to pay the rowers.

Here we stand on Bali shore faced with the problem of finding shelter for the night. We telephone about to neighbouring places, and are parted from our American friends, who, against their will, have to charter a car and drive to Kintamani to find shelter against the fast-coming night. We will be able to get a room at Gitgit. The cars move on; we wave, they wave, and in the gathering dusk we climb the hilly lands, alighting at last because the hills are too steep. Some natives carry our luggage—giantesque silhouettes against the almost dark sky. At last we arrive.

A bath, a cup of tea, restore us. The heat is gone now, the terraced ricefields on the hills are lost in the vague mist, the trees which line them rise in quiet beauty and the blue sea vanishes into the dusk.

We have been absorbed by the land of gods and ghosts, of temples and feasts of offering.

"Offerings, Bali" *(Drypoint)*

Chapter Twenty Seven

Bali

EARLY the next morning we are out to enjoy the wide landscape which scintillates in the bright sunlight, and the glorious view from the cupola of the Government resthouse entices us to a stroll between the ricefields and the overgrown hills to a near-by waterfall. At a temple yard with a quaint gateway which seems to have been split open, we admire the beautifully carved doors and curious images of ghosts. Along the narrow footpath dogs yelp at us; poor thin beasts they are such as Bali possesses in thousands. Yonder a boy tends the fine Bali cattle, perfectly at ease in what is to us the roasting heat of the sun.

At Singaradja, the port, it is, if possible, warmer. The loitering stranger—and at that temperature there is nothing for it but to loiter—soon finds himself the prey of a Balinese who inquires whether he is interested in woodcarvings or silver statuettes. If one follows the native it is to some private house, and everywhere stand the evidences of the vivid imagination which creates ghosts and gods everywhere and at all times. At the gate of each house square pillars stand having open niches for the gods; or the niches are let into the wall which surrounds the property; or consoles serve the same high purpose. Is there not charm in a country where the gods come and rest awhile, leave their eternal purposes in the Empyrean to take possession of such earthly niches and absorb the scent of the flowers and fruit wherewith the owner of the house delights to welcome them?

Everywhere in Bali the wanderer finds little houses for the gods. The peasant is both architect and sculptor. He builds his tiny temple, and when it decays he abandons it to its fate and builds and carves another. We Occidentals preserve and scrupulously save; the Balinese airily allows his buildings to crumble and

125

An Artist in the Tropics

creates anew, like Michael Angelo, who broke down his earlier work to make room for grander achievements.

A rice shed, generally a delicate wooden building, is adorned with the most elegant matting ornaments of split and twisted bamboo; long, slender and graceful as some fantastic lanterns, or round ones with protruding points and plumes to left and right like the winged wheel of the sun.

High on its poles the shed stands, and beneath it the swine find a shadowed place where they jostle each other. In the general oriental carelessness and dirt typical of every yard, women sit and weave of purple silk and gold thread materials in conventional designs of unsurpassed beauty.

No yard lacks a god's resthouse, and offerings of rice and flowers are to be seen everywhere. To the temples offerings of great beauty are carried, sometimes high structures of bamboo covered with bright red and yellow fruits arranged to form ornaments. They are borne along the sun-scorched road by women who carry them on their heads. When in the dusk some prayers have been said, and incense has been burned and water sprinkled, the eatables are taken home again, for by happy chance, the gods only live on the scent.

Long rows of women pass continually along the roads, carrying market goods with stately, regal poise. The dark sarong covers a brighter one beneath; the upper part of the body is uncovered. The Dutch may blush to realise that the jacket, which some narrow-minded official once tried to force on the guileless natives, is only thrown over their bodies when—white people draw near. The Balinese woman then throws the sleeves over her shoulders backwards, but this stupid custom will, one hopes, soon die out as Time throws its own little curtain of forgetfulness over the behest of the officious Dutch gentleman.

Bali, state the guide books, covers only one sixth of the area of the Netherlands, but they make no computation of the overwhelming proportion of dogs which it boasts. As soon as one leaves the mainroads and essays a footpath, a yard, a temple-court, a dozen of these beasts are at one's heels, shrieking, barking, yelping, howling as only the dogs of Bali can. Against their unceasing din there is no hope of enjoying the sublime mood engendered by the stately waringin trees. At one place a great number of these half-

Bali

wild village dogs, belonging to nobody, were killed, and a real boon it must have been both to the poor, sick, miserable animals themselves and to the humans of that environ. Perhaps these innumerable beasts are a dispensation of Providence to put to the test the tourist's genuineness in his enthusiasm for the island, for they cause many visitors to stay in their automobiles and so leave the life of Bali, its arts and crafts intact. Which, for a country so threatened by the disaster of becoming a fashion as Bali, must be a real boon.

Other factors combine to protect Bali and its arts from a plethora of popularity. There is hardly any accommodation for travellers and no comforts; hardly any motor cars, the *sine qua non* of existence to the dilettante tourists of the East, without which nothing can be seen. To most tourists it will not sound inviting that the boys in a resthouse not only use a serviette to clean the plates, but also use it for those functions where your European finds a handkerchief a valuable asset. The fastidious, therefore, will be well advised to stay at home. Moreover, the roads are seldom used, and if here or there something goes wrong with your car no help is likely to be forthcoming.

To one who is not afraid of walking for some hours in the fierce glow of the tropical sun, a temple with its fairy ornamentation, its blossoming trees, its atmosphere of divinity and beauty will compensate for these little discomforts on the material plane. The places where the dead are burned are set with magical trees, which seem to house ghosts and gods and to express the sinister powers of which these are the avowed possessors.

That a burning is to take place shortly is apparent from the high structure of bamboo, the badé, in which the corpses are carried to the spot. These towers, exuberantly coloured with ornaments in paper, giltwork, paintings and the like, are abundantly adorned. Predominant among the colours flash those significant of Trimurti, Brahma, Vishnu and Shiva: red, white, and black or blue.

The high tower has a foundation of immense bamboo sticks which scores of carriers bear on their shoulders, transporting the bodies from the house to the burning field. We saw the procession on the main road—a great crowd, bawling, shouting, running, in clouds of dust—and tremendously high above it the airy tower sparkling in a riot of bright colours against the green, the marvellous apex of this barbaric procession, this demoniac Feast of the Dead.

An Artist in the Tropics

A priest running in front leads the way; he holds a long rope fastened to the tower, as tacking and turning he causes the procession to run about, suddenly twisting back upon its own track, veering to this side, then to that, so that the evil spirits who are thought to be on the alert to take possession of the body may be put off the track.

A wild shouting accompanied a new phase of the ritual. With full force the carriers lift their rods higher until all have their arms stretched taut above their heads, forming an archway under which some who seem to be relations of the deceased rapidly pass several times to and fro. Then again the throng continues on its way.

We find it difficult to keep pace with their speed, but already some things were familiar to us, for in the morning we have taken the opportunity of looking round, and have seen the many coffins of carved wood, cut in the shape of elephants—the makara—and of bulls —the nandi. At the burning festivals several dead are brought together to the hill of the ceremony; the assembled coffins glitter in the sun.

The wonderful, strange, wildly beating funeral music, which went on day and night along the road, reaches its climax at the hill; it breaks forth in heavy, torturing rhythms, a sinister *marche funèbre*.

A ladder is raised against the brilliant tower. In a wild rush the bodies are brought down, and, in a whirl of shouting men, raced towards the coffins and put to rest. The scene is frenzy itself as they tear down and fling about the adornments of the tower so carefully painted and shaped, immediately its precious burden of bodies has been taken from it. Then the tremendous structure is lit. Flaming and crackling the dry bamboo is soon a column of fire as from some awful dream, until it tumbles smokily into the débris of smouldering sticks and particles.

Meantime a priest has detached himself from the throng. He mutters for the last time his prayers for the welfare of the dead. Long are the nails of his left hand, as long as the fingers themselves. He passes on from coffin to coffin performing the rites. Some of the coffins contain only skeletons, for the long and costly preparations, the feasts and ceremonies of a burning often necessitate the dead being buried first and exhumed for the day of the Great Fire. It appears as if for the last time care of the body is taken, as a movement

On the Way to the Temple, Bali (*Drawing*)

Bali

of combing the hair is made before a mirror held up to the head. When all is finished the mirror is held again that the dead may see that all has been done well.

Holy water is carried in earthenware pots by long files of women; the priest will sprinkle it over the bodies, the pots be broken to pieces and flowers scattered in the coffins. A payong should be held over his head, but if this be not forthcoming an ordinary umbrella will suit the purpose, and shade his grey hair tied together in a bunch on the top of his head. Slowly he opens some folded manuscripts and puts them in the coffins, together with a little board on which the human form is drawn.

Now some dancers advance and perform a dance of combat with long lances. In their crude black and white paint they seem to us to symbolise the eternal strife between good and evil.

The end of the formal ceremonies draws near. Wood is carried on and piled around the coffin-animals and between their legs. They seem to be a vehicle to the dead as the gods themselves have their animal vehicles. A shower of Chinese coppers—the coin which, with one silver Dutch coin, constitutes the entire currency of Bali—are thrown to the crowds, and grown-ups and children scramble to catch as many as they can as the coins fly from the long strings which have held them together through their pierced centres.

Now, at last, the backs of the coffin-beasts are put into place, forming the lids. With a great crackling and the spurting of little clouds of smoke they begin to burn. Charred legs crumble and amid the increasing flames the carven animals sink with a strange reality of their own, their eyes big and round, their heads lifted for a little above the devouring flames. Widening, heightening, glowing, unbearable, the consuming fire takes its toll of the Dead.

Feasts are numerous in Bali.

The Javanese are submissive; the Balinese exuberant. Especially in Southern Bali one often finds the roads adorned with rows of long bamboo poles to which flags and brightly coloured pennants are tied. The thin bamboo end bends gracefully, and from it depends one of the marvellously elegant pieces of interwoven cane which the Balinese love to use as ornaments in temples, courts and houses. The colours of the flags transform the whole village into a gay avenue along which hundreds crowd to the house of the feast. Four great

An Artist in the Tropics

living tortoises lie there, their legs tethered; heavy, motionless as stones beneath their shields, they would serve for the festival meal. Many women, beautifully dressed, bring in delicacies and ornaments as gifts to the feast and the feasting place; music is being played as they come.

All through the village the spirit of carnival is abroad; everywhere is a blaze of colour, liveliness, laughter, movement and joy. Girls have scented flowers in their hair, processions pass by, and when we inquire what is the occasion of the feast an old woman gives that best of all reasons, that the people are just "senang hati," which is to say, glad of heart.

This is in the South of Bali, most typical of the nation. In the central part of the island, where the immense mountains rise, one cannot imagine that one is in the tropics. The land is cool and bare; on the ridge of the watershed running east and west lies the village Kintamani, with glorious panoramas although the plain itself whereon it stands is entirely barren and solitary. Fierce winds prevent the growth of trees. The wild Batoor, the giant volcano, towers above the hilly lands, the everlasting clouds about its craters. Over against it stand the Goonoong Agoong and the Peak of Bali, giants all in this austere landscape.

From Kintamani one looks down on the blue lake of Batoor, if the clouds and mists have not enveloped it. Then rain storms will come, and happy is the traveller who reaches the sheltering guest house in time. The hills beneath us are veiled in the rolling clouds, Mount Batoor appears only in blurred vagueness now and then; one might be on some other planet or on the lifeless plains of the moon . . . until suddenly the imagination is disturbed by a little group of trippers who have been caught by the storm. They are all soaked and have nothing to change into. Everything suits the purpose on such an occasion: my pyjamas clothe a government official, a jacket and a blanket provide another gentleman's costume, and a glass of warm wine, to counter the cold mountain atmosphere, puts everything in pleasant perspective. The little rest-house where we two are the only guests is soon very lively.

Later in the day, when the rain stops and their clothes are dried again, the party leave. We also go out for a walk across the bare, unprotected lands. Pale mists glide over Batoor lake and splashes of sunshine float across it. The wide lands are an iridescent

"A CREMATION, BALI"

K

Bali

landscape of dream, mysterious, bewitched and barren in the changing light.

Sunrise the next morning is yet another dream of beauty. Intense purple-black is the whole vast contour of Mount Batoor, its threatening cone against the lightening skies where float the first tints of blue and pink. Brighter yellow and radiant orange break through the massed clouds, till at last the sun itself swings over the horizon, raying in full glory.

It was a sunrise such as we had seldom seen, even though here in the East they are so often almost terrible in their loveliness. An artist stands aghast as Nature handles her vast palette with her own unbounded liberty, and we think of Whistler's stricture upon the "unbearable" sunsets of Europe and wonder what he would have said of these.

Two things constitute Bali's glory. The first is that the land is of a nature and structure which can be apprehended and therefore enjoyed. It has mountains and great views, certainly, but not so many of the one nor so vast as to the other as one finds in Java or Sumatra, so that the landscape is more intimate, more endearingly proportioned to man. The second charm of Bali is—that there are so few Europeans. Bali's beauty and life form a unity which manifests itself in buildings and temples as it does nowhere else in the East Indies. Jealously we would guard that unspoiled beauty, protect it from the conscious vulgarity of such posters as we saw there boosting Somebody's Tyres in crude colouring and bad lettering, and from such unconscious error as that of the open air museum erected some twelve or fourteen years ago to immortalise the various architectural styles of South Bali. The intention was doubtless excellent, but entirely superfluous. A Balinese builds a temple if he has a desire to honour his gods; he builds a house if he has a desire to live in the particular place where he builds it. The innermost thoughts of the Balinese invited by the European Government to build a temple where he could not worship and a house where he could not live, can only be surmised if we imagine a European erecting a railway station where no train would come and a church where no service would ever be. Nevertheless, we met those who could not see the Balinese objection to the strange proceeding.

An Artist in the Tropics

Since Bali's temples are live centres of worship all over the island, Bali's sculpture alive in its abundant fascination, the museum stands as an open grave for the arts of the island, waiting for the time when our mechanical civilisation will have killed Bali's soul.

It is to be hoped that the Government or, to be precise, the Resident at Bali, will be able to keep the island inviolate from this Philistinism. It is small, and the task could be performed. It would be an excellent first step if His Honour the Resident had the first poster hoarding taken away for ever.

A Temple-Gate, Bali *(Etching)*

Chapter Twenty Eight

Makassar

WHY has the name of Makassar always stood for us as the symbol of a town with many gateways, porches, coloured pageants, with crowded, teeming markets, mysteriously shuttered palaces of Sultans and silent mosques? Why must we learn daily and regularly that the Orient of the fancy and the Orient of tropical fact are not the same? Why is it so difficult to rid ourselves of the old way of seeing as we learned it in Europe, and so acquire genius for seeing the Indies in the Indian way, looking strangely empty by the mere superabundance of light, the enormous plains not veiled in any atmospheric beauty, but clear, distinct, sharply defined? After Java, now again on this island of Celebes the cruel tropic sun has burned away all subtlety, all charm and modesty which would make this town of Makassar even more attractive than it already is. For the glare of the light kills all the Arabian Nights romance of the lanes with their widely-rooted canari-trees and thin-leaved tamarinds, which lead from the busy beach to the quiet countryside.

In the Chinese quarter the yellow Asiatics practise all conceivable forms of craftsmanship, and in the heavy shadows of the workshops they catch on their dim golden bodies hardly a glint of the hard brightness of the streets. Industriously they handle the hard wood, they saw and hammer and cut the planks to shape, construct carriages, cases, furniture. In their busy hands the iron glitters and the brass shines, and furtively they glance at the foreigner who saunters through their crowded streets.

The sea and proas' beach are one immense glitter. The stranded vessels have the appearance of strange sea monsters thrown ashore at high tide. From these narrow proas the brown, strong arms carry baskets full of golden manggas[1] and loads of quaint fish,

[1]Manggas : a fruit.

An Artist in the Tropics

marvellously spotted and striped in endless variety of colours. In the evening, as silence falls with the short twilight, some porpoises tumble and splash with a curious babble of soft sound. Then darkness, the softening darkness, descends, veils the outlines of the fortress Rotterdam, and we forget that in the daylight it looks like a bit of Old Holland without that intimacy which makes the original so dear to us. But it is mere imitation, a kind of exhibition model of its original, placed, forgotten and left where it now stands. The moat is dry and has been so for years. A footpath leads from it to the beach where big jars filled with drinking water are carried on board the boats on brown, bent backs or swaying bamboo poles. The fisherman on the wide blue seas will draw his drink from them. In the glare of daylight there is little romance, none of the thousand-and-one-nights enchantment. The East has a beauty of its own, a tyrannical beauty, severe, cruel, all-embracing. No Northern mists here, such as give our own lands their infinite variety of moods and enrich the European landscape with the poetry and reflect for us the evasive subtleties of our own feelings; no dew falls. Clouds there are in the mountain regions. On the plains the sky is clear blue or unbroken grey. A palm stands stiff and straight, etched in hard line against the unvaried sky. A short dusk—then absolute night. The blue waters no longer scintillate like some exquisite cloisonné, but the whimsical dancing of fire-flies begins, and everywhere is heard the loud shrilling of the beetles and of the myriad thousands of crickets.

The flaming red and purple worn by the Makassars is lost in the darkness wherein bats flutter gruesomely; and all the weird noises of the night-marauding beasts commence. A dead calm lies over all the vegetation, but the air is full of the movement of a million insects.

We meditate: after Java with its three nations—Soondanese, Javanese, Madurese, each with their own language—we get to know the Makassars, another race, wild as the sea, a new tongue, a new, angular script. Farther into the island here are the Booginese, the Toradjas—no end of new names, new nations, new customs. All are foreigners to one another; foreign in language, race, habits, character, religion, daily ways. The Balinese in Bali again are inhabitants of a separate world; Lombok, the next island, inhabited by Sassaks; the interminable list goes on. The variety of the nations is

Makassar

as striking as the unity of nature, and of both we have hitherto had but a vague notion, approximating but slightly to the real facts.

If, after a long period, we begin to feel at home in the East, if we no longer horribly miss the familiar things which these lands lack, as we get accustomed to vast proportions wherein a great group of trees, which at home would dominate a landscape, are but a trifle in the immensity of nature, then a wave of fear steals over us for the little country we have left: its little bridges, its little trees, its little canals and little gabled houses, its ditches and fences, its little proprieties and little ideas.

One enormous, brutal force of nature is here, quiescent it may be at night, but always present, always felt, always perceptible and potent.

When day returns again the grand sweep of the décor of this immense stage awaits us. Panorama after panorama it shows us as by magic; conjures up newer, vaster vistas as we go; causes mountains to rise and valleys and plains to undulate. Everything is plastic, sculptural; from near to the far horizon everything is equally luminous, equally clear and defined, shining distinctly in the unwavering light.

Chapter Twenty Nine

Banyermasin

To Borneo! The strange, unknown, almost untrodden land of virgin woods, enormous rivers, and head-hunting Dayaks. Land of illusion to the many who dreamed of gold and treasure, and went to find—nothing. We "blandas" may be the governing race and may speak of ourselves in the exaltation of the third person when we speak Malay, but the inhabitants do not give more information than they wish to the merchant adventurers. Diligently the native goldsmith, the "tookang-mas", toils on at his craft, whilst in the endless woods the enterprises of the white seekers, unaided beneath the curse of his "ca' canny", quietly rust away to dust and powder.

We reach an estuary as wide as a sea, but lesser and lesser it becomes as we move up the immense river. The horizon closes in upon us. To left and right a close hedge of nippa rises out of the water; marsh-palms they are, low and fan-shaped. It seems an impenetrable tangle, but here and there a big trunk of a tree lies in the water moored to some palm, and occasionally a naked human form bestrides it. It is a native who lives near by in the marsh, and uses the tree which has drifted down the river from the far inland mountains as a fortuitous bathing board, despite the hundreds of alligators with which the rivers abound. He lives a primitive Bushman existence. A few Dayaks are also on board as passengers; they are like cats, their bodies are yellow, supple, their ears are distorted, the lobes coming down nearly to the shoulder. They slide down the side of the ship for a bath. Heavy black hair is long on their backs and hangs to the waist. Sinuous and lithe as panthers, they seem prehistoric and subhuman.

Higher palms now rise out of the fringe of low nippa. Now and again a wooden shed, a dwelling, is built over the water on high

RIVER CRAFT (*Drawing*)

Banyermasin

poles; now and again we see a proa, a hollowed tree-trunk boat, then more and more rivercraft, quick boats of finer shape. In the sharp turns of the river our steamer seems to touch the banks now, but occasionally it opens out into a wider pool where a large Madurese vessel may glide past without a sound.

Then Banyermasin appears: real ships, the paraphernalia of a port. We step ashore, and here, among the virgin woods of Borneo, we find ourselves in Holland. Immediately before us as we leave the boat is an ordinary Dutch letterbox, painted grey in the horrible sinister colour of a man-of-war. It stands to greet us formally; Dutch, imperturbable and plain. The road itself, the town, are these not Dutch too? The houses are connected with the roadway by small bridges, painted white, the railings severe and straight as in our own picturesque country. Is this an old Dutch village or is it indeed Borneo? Who would not recognise the Dutch humour of the notice above the prison gate, the laconic "No admittance" which is so very, very Dutch? There is surely no other country in the world where access is forbidden so abundantly as in Holland, and as soon as we see that notice we feel even more at home than when the good old letter-box greeted us greyly on the landing stage.

Certain things, however, are not Dutch. The prisoners, for example. They come walking down the road in single file, each holds in his own hand the rope which is the symbol of his imprisonment in naïve admission of that fact. They smoke the native cigarette, the inseparable "strootje",[1] they laugh, they chat, they do not care in the least. Being condemned is to most natives a thing which happens occasionally, not a matter for shame or fear, nor even for depression. Their chief duty seems to be that of cutting the grass at the roadside.

But the river, the water, is really the town of Banyermasin. From bank to bank, upstream, downstream, from creek to creek the boats swarm. Long and cranked "tambangans" flash past, quickly paddled and then arrested and slowly swaying; with a single stroke the paddleman turns them round, miraculously escaping a collision with great lumps of wood, torn off in storms and washed down the river from the mountainous hinterland. Most of these are overgrown with water-plants since they started their journey down

[1]Strootje : Literally, little straw, because the tobacco is kept together by dried leaf, hard and yellow, like straw.

An Artist in the Tropics

the long rivers. Floating concessions they are called, and we dare to reflect that these are not the only concessions which have gone adrift in this land.

Japanese and Chinese steamers enter the deep waters, and like strange sea-birds the brightly painted, carved boats of the Madurese lie side by side with the heavy Occidental ocean boats. All this busy river life, with its endless variety of native river craft, Banyermasin presents to us as our gondolier paddles us on and on into creeks and innumerable backwaters of the vast river.

Chapter Thirty

Balikpapan: Oil Town

BALIKPAPAN is the capital of the Batavian Petroleum Maatschappij (Company), the B.P.M. It is and has everything there. Its own grounds, own tanks, own boats, shops, works, lawn-tennis courts— even its own time. The omnipotent company puts the Balikpapan clocks as it wishes to indicate time—a super-Americanism to the Dutch mind.

Everywhere there is oil, everywhere oilpipes. The raw product sometimes comes from places miles and miles away. Conduit tubes burrow through the ground; pipes lie over the ground; there is oil along the roads, oil in the bathroom, oil on the bathing water. That at least has practical advantages, since it prevents the mosquitos from breeding in the water as they now can do only in the one tiny part without oil, the communicating casks cut off with a concrete fence from the main basin. The mention of the bath prompts the memory that the usual method of bathing in the East is to stand in front of the basin and taking pailfuls of the water to pour them one by one over the body. This is assumed to give a cooler bath than the Occidental way, and does not demand so much water, which is often a matter of importance in the Indies. The oil in the bathroom by its joint discouragement of the mosquito birth rate and of super-fluous bathing thus has two practical advantages; but what is not practical in oil-town?

The roads scorn the sentimental method of naming and in this America-in-miniature bear numbers. "Djalan", which is to say Road, 6, or 10, or 47. You cannot possibly make an error, and the completeness of the system is the more remarkable in the Indies where often roads have no name or indication at all. Here every-thing has a number: a steam tram is B.P.M. 3; a tank-boat, B.P.M. 12.

An Artist in the Tropics

One begins to wonder why the men have escaped the universal numeration.

Everything is produced on the spot. Here are the works and factories where wooden oil barrels are made, there the works and factories where iron ones are made; yonder the sulphuric acid works, for sulphuric acid is used to purify the raw oil. Natives of all thinkable races are employed, many "imported" coolies. One type of man has been found best for transporting purposes, another for this, a third for that. Organisation under your feet, and organisation over your head, a strange growth in the very heart of the far-spreading, virgin forests.

The coast line forms an almost immeasurable bay, and along the bay runs a wide, main road. For the most part it has had to be cut through the hills; it is carefully planted with widely-branched "flamboyant" trees, beloved for their flame-red, sparkling blossoms. The side-roads have fine tjemaras—needle-leaved trees—or high palms. They lead to villages of wooden country houses on poles, well-built and hygienic, and behind these lie the hills affording a fine view over the large bay with its smooth, bright waters extending beyond the field of vision.

The oil-shafts and wells lie far away in the woods. Such a boring ground is that called "Louise" near the native village of Sanga Sanga Dalem. It is a tiny harbour, a tiny village street, a tiny shop, a tiny club-house. Now and then a billiard match breaks the hermit-like existence of the village. Hardly ever is a performance or a concert possible in such isolation. Boring towers stand along the riverside for an enormous distance. Through the wild over-grown marshes pipes conduct the oil to oil-town, Balikpapan; through wild woods they pass, nightmare woods of rotten trunks and branches, of twisted, distorted nature, blighted and made horrible because of the oil which covers the water.

Farther on again another oilfield, Sambodya, an endless stream of oil pumping eternally from the earth. Sometimes the rivers are as wide as lakes. From the flat, smooth surface of the water the wooded banks rise as incredibly as a realistic decoration from the planks of a stage floor.

If luck is with you it may take some six hours to arrive from Sanga Sanga Dalem to Sambodya. But the little tug which brings you there (B.P.M. 32) often has to escort tanks, boats or rafts.

A Bay, Borneo (Drawing)

Balikpapan: Oil Town

Whereupon you may not catch the tide that takes you over one of the numerous sandbanks which abound in the wide rivers here. You wait several hours. If you share our fate you will take twenty-four hours doing the six hours' trip, and this upon a primitive tug which has no food on board. When at last the vessel reaches its destination you must have no illusion that you have yet arrived at Sambodya. With bag and baggage the passengers disembark into rowing boats, and thus make the shore after half an hour's vigorous rowing. But not Sambodya, for at the bank is nothing more tangible than the terminus of the steam tram. If the tram happens to be there one can proceed without further delay through the great, untouched forests, where all thinkable animals must be lurking although happily one doesn't see them, for another solid hour. This again is minimum time, for it may chance that now and again it is commandeered to bring uphill some waggon laden with timber, iron, pipes or other essential B.P.M. need. If the load proves too heavy it will just be deserted at the roadside, from whence nobody is likely to steal it. But this again takes time, and just when you have given up all human hope of ever arriving, you arrive. You discover an open space in the dense vegetation, covered with the type of wooden house already mentioned, and you alight to B.P.M. 27, 28, or what you will. Oil pipes are everywhere; pink pipes, bleached red pipes, just as you have met them in the capital Balikpapan.

If the aim of this pilgrimage is a concert you will find that Sambodya has its compensations in the form of the appreciation of these people of the solitudes as compared with many a blasé European audience. The pianist will play with just as much pleasure on a very virgin-wood piano here because of that appreciation, as on the very best concert grand yonder. A Polish boring engineer may get so excited at this memory-evoking European music that he will continue to sing Polish songs until deep into the night, though nobody present knows one syllable of Polish, however much they may be enchanted by his exalted appearance and the curls of his long moustache which touches his ears.

The next day the travellers return the same long, long way. The vessel is waiting at the roadstead, will, indeed, wait with Oriental patience any length of time until the musicians return. The path through the woods, which we now travel by steam tram, had to be

An Artist in the Tropics

negotiated on horseback until a few years ago. Thus the B.P.M. ambition, the B.P.M. energy is ameliorating, improving everywhere and everything, restlessly, endlessly. It is the same intense activity which the Dutch appreciate in the Americans: the same systematic organisation which has caused many a Dutch scientist to become so absorbed in the organisation of the practice of his science that he has allowed no time for scientific work himself.

After untold hours we are back in Balikpapan, and then we pass on. It would seem that oil-town has even organised its last impression, a farewell gesture of its ceaseless activity. From the passenger deck of the steamer "Tasman" bound for Australia, we look down on a pier where a tower-high mass of oil tins suffers demolition at the hands of bearded Orientals. With systematic liveliness the enormous quantity is brought into the steamer. The hold swallows tin after tin, and tin after tin proclaims: B.P.M., B.P.M., B.P.M.

MALAY HOUSES, PALEMBANG (*Etching*)

Chapter Thirty One

Palembang, South Sumatra

FROM Batavia, the capital of Java, it takes a night, a day and yet another night by boat. A grey sky and a grey sea, or a blue sky and a blue sea. Perhaps a vague line along the horizon may indicate the island of Banka. Nothing is Oriental save the heat in that voyage, and when we arrive at an ordinary landing stage there is nothing Oriental either. The town rewards us, however; it is one of the most picturesque in the archipelago.

The mighty river of which it lines both banks is, as in Borneo, alive with innumerable boats rowing and sailing in all directions. Shops are built upon rafts, and even houses. Beneath the rafts lie crocodiles awaiting their prey. Everywhere is creek and canal; all houses stand upon poles since at high tide nearly all the ground is inundated. Here and there we have a little bridge.

As the main hotel is being renewed, we stay in wooden houses on the outskirts of the town where the land rises a little. Our lodging happens to be next door to a depot for wild animals belonging to a man who supplies these to menageries and zoological gardens. Five elephants walk around, some five or six tigers roar in their wooden cages. The proprietor assures us that these are strong enough to transport the animals in, and as they leap at us with open mouths, their claws tearing the woodwork, we hope that his faith is justified. The elephants are quieter guests. A few of them have a place on a hill where they are tied to strong trees. There are some old, forgotten graves there, their richly carved railings almost perished, but to these the pachyderms cannot get. So they tear branches from the trees and blow at each other, smashing them to pieces the next moment as they throw them away, like destructive boys. In the evening they are carefully towed home. One big

An Artist in the Tropics

rope is eased off slowly, the other drawn in at the same rate, and when they have been thus guided into their wooden cages every one of them, together with its cage, is tied carefully to a big tree; then they are at anchor safely.

A motor-launch brings us up the river occasionally, where many a Chinese drawing of market-goers in a boat passes by. Our guide, an official, introduces us to the richest Chinese of the town. We stroll along the narrow footpaths of the Venice of the East, as people of the Indies choose to call it—a Venice, it must be confessed, rather dirty, colourless and muddy. The plain wooden houses are still duller in colour in the excessive light of the Orient than they would be in our hemisphere. We lounge over the railings of bridges, look on at the markets where the coarse pottery is sold, but more interesting is the Chinese interior. Unfortunately the Orientals of all nations like to imitate the Western culture of the most dubious standards with which they come into contact, so that apart from a big safe we find Victorian furniture and whatnots, consoles, with vases and so forth, and on the wall some old steel engravings. At home we dispense with this type of wall decoration; but here the products of a period when people had leisure to engrave in steel the horrors and sentimentalities of our "movies" are still highly approved, and we have the "Tendres Adieux" wherein a gentlemanly dragoon salutes with chaste kiss some clinging maiden, hanging fraternally side by side with the realistically depicted slaughter of some mediæval duke.

More truly Chinese was the house which a number of Chinese families shared. Silent courts, closed in by silent houses, had palms and squares and fountains, and in the halls beautifully carved, ancient furniture stood, proud and dignified, as though awaiting the arrival of a king.

As we pass on we see everywhere the houses standing in the mud and accessible only by planks. Then the launch brings us to the river again, where all sorts of articles were proffered for sale in the little stalls on the rafts. We halted at a place with magnificently painted hats made of dried palm leaves, serving as protection against rain and sun alike, and having the size of small umbrellas adequately to fulfil this dual task, not only for the wearer's head but also for his shoulders.

Their hurdle work is exquisite, the strips overlapping each other like tiles on a roof, and then carefully sewed and painted red,

Palembang, South Sumatra

black and gilt. Off we go with the finest of them all in our possession. Our treasure proved to be rather cumbersome when we got it on the launch; and even larger, when, arrived at our starting place at the pier, we tried to get into the carriage with it. We could get in, but not so our beautiful hat, which had to hang overboard and when we came to the hotel no case was large enough to hold our new purchase. Whereupon we had to give the "Mandoor", the head-boy, a ruinous tip to buy a case somewhere. It proved that the case cost as much as the hat itself, and as we faced the fact that we had yet to pay freight to Batavia, and from Batavia to Holland, we realised that we artists are an improvident race and our enthusiasms greater than our business sense. This was certainly the most costly hat we had ever bought in our lives, and, we meditated, would cost us our lives as well if we dared to wear it in the streets of our native town as we should probably be stoned to death by riotous gutter urchins.

Chapter Thirty Two

Across South Sumatra

On the map the distance between Palembang and Benkoolen does not look great, but of no country is the map so flattering as of Sumatra. In the south-east are impenetrable marshes of enormous size, and along the west coast runs an almost inaccessible mountain ridge across which a few seemingly impossible roads have been constructed with infinite pains. A railway is available for the first stretch only. The train leaves at six a.m.; at a quarter to five one leaves the hotel to get the boat upstream to the station. Ergo, a cart with the luggage should leave at about four; and ergo again, an early morning. But natives can be punctual and we only asked them to be there a quarter of an hour before the time appointed; not later, we impressed, not later.

In the middle of the night as it seemed to us a great knocking and shouting woke us: they were there. Our watches said a quarter to three; the men said a quarter to four, sure, sure. What can one do in such a case? We get up, dress, sigh, yawn, and pack our handbags, and away the men go with everything. Now we must wait for the little carriage which will convey us to the boat. We sit and wait. Silence, dead silence. No carriage. Must we walk? Must we leave behind all provision for a journey of almost a day? Everybody, everything sleeps. We hesitate on the threshold. Suddenly steps approach, and the hotel manager appears, having come to wake us and being staggered to see us ready to depart.

"You have yet an hour," he assures us. "What on earth made you stir so early? And your barang[1] already gone! A full hour you have."

[1]Barang : Luggage.

A PADDLAR (Drawing)

Across South Sumatra

We accept our fate miserably, but the manager soon returns with a cup of coffee to cheer us and help us pass the dismal hour of waiting.

At last our carriage arrives. We begin the trip as though we were going to a funeral, but not to such a cheery one as the native and Chinese funerals which we had so often seen pass—loudly chattering and laughing processions as they are, with a throng of gesticulating men following the body which is carried on a bier and covered with a poor or richly embroidered pall according to the circumstances of the deceased.

Our carriage jolts on while we try to master our sleepiness by such sleepy contemplations, and then, just when sleep itself is mastering us, we arrive at the landing stage. Black night everywhere. Human forms appear in the dim light of the lamps of the incoming boat; they stand near or sit amid the confusion of waiting baggage. Hastily everybody drags his belongings on board, and off we go. Then a silent journey is followed by a landing just as hurried, a dragging off of baggage, cases, bags and parcels. In the darkness everybody makes a stumbling way between sandhills, loose rails, carts, switches. Like mosquitos we all direct ourselves towards a light in the distance which indicates the probable site of the station. At last we are in the train, and after all these eventualities and journeys our real journey begins, and happily the day begins to dawn.

Together with the rising of the sun our spirits rise. The hours slowly pass. The railroad is closed in by impenetrable vegetation all the time. After about eight hours we are at the other end, Mooara Enim; and the resthouse is the only thing we have any interest in.

The village of Mooara Enim is little more than a place where the product of the wild woods, rattan, is brought and sent on to the coast by train. Some dozens of Europeans live here supervising the construction of the railway onwards. Slowly it advances through the barely populated, thickly wooded, mountainous land, where elephants, tigers and snakes abound.

Only sporadically a traveller passes here. The one public means of conveyance is the automobile service, which carries the mails and goes to Benkoolen on the west coast in a three days' journey. A short cut, however, taken in a private car might make it possible to cross the wild country in one day, though nobody can be sure whether the by-roads are inaccessible by reason of trees struck

An Artist in the Tropics

down in tropical storms or sections washed away in the torrents which rush down the mountain slopes. We risked it. Taking three days would mean missing the boat which calls once a week only at Benkoolen, and thereby the loss of six days, and so we decided on the wild dash along the short cut.

Hour after hour we raced along through the mountains entirely covered with thick vegetation, clearing a distance of 200 miles. The driver, a native chauffeur, is a miracle worker. He drives without the least hesitation over giddily winding roads, which curl and twist endlessly along the mountain side. It seems an uninterrupted world of forests; whole mountains are one thick, curly mass of green; there is no cessation. The roads are narrow—a car from the other direction with a careless driver would mean an inevitable smash and both automobiles over into the vertical abysses which flank the road. Soon rain pours down. An explosion signifies a burst tyre, and we draw the car up between the deep ravine and the vegetation close as a hedge from which a wild howling of apes resounds and moves towards us. A heavy bass preludes every outburst of the whole shrieking pack; then they are gone, and only the everlasting chirping of the crickets breaks the primeval silence.

The rain begins again, and soon the road becomes a river. We make two more halts to push the car out of places as muddy as deep ditches. On again we rush alongside the ravines, till in the darkness of the falling night we discover lights in the distance: our destination. But before we reach them we have another halt. Some screw or other is gone, and in the darkness our driver lies under the car, the rain splashes, the whole car is soaked and so are we. So in the evening we arrive hungry, thirsty, nerve-sick of the dangers of that perilous journey, wet, and dead beat with fatigue.

Then comes the hotel manager to explain that he has no room for us. Even the passage is not available as it has already been commandeered for a bedroom. We can only proceed and hope for accommodation at some Chinese restaurant. We scrape together the remnant of our energy and decide that we will occupy the front verandah, will sit there through the night in our wet clothes rather than go on searching, whether the manager likes it or not. In the meantime the guests have gathered about the two wet people; they stand in an interested circle around the puddles which we make, and before long a gentleman has offered us his room and volunteered

ON THE RIVER, SUMATRA   *(Etching)*

Across South Sumatra

to share that of another. So we occupy his apartment where he has left his sixteen pairs of boots and shoes and all his other belongings at the mercy of the strangers to whom he has played the Good Samaritan.

This is the beginning of the little town of Benkoolen, and it is almost the end of it, for its tale is soon told. It is an insignificant place where about sixty Europeans live. There is no liveliness of Eastern markets as at east coast Palembang, the Venice of the Mud, but only a hilly coast, facing the enormous seas which stretch unbroken from here to the South Pole.

Yet it was at this isolated and unlikely place that the whole mysteries of the world were revealed to us. Who would not have come through those hundreds of miles of discomforts, risked the dangers of the ravines, the rains and tropic heat, to sit at the feet of the Russian as we did and hear the world's motives and motive forces unfolded in broken English with much emphasis and greater length? Things which have puzzled all the thinkers of the centuries were crystal clear. It really was so simple.

The Christian aim is purely that of love; therefore, the Anti-Christian aim is Hate and Evil. He may not even realise it, but so it is. The Jew in Russia, the Mongol in Asia, the Turk in the Balkans, the Negro in Africa, all aim at war because they are not Christians. We inquired whether there was not some suggestion that the last world war was carried on by the Christians versus Christians, but were assured that it was all worked by the Anti-Christians. Not only did they make war among themselves, but so thoroughly possessed were they by evil forces that they were able to make even the good Christians fight one another. That is why the Christian world must organise against the Anti-Christ, and according to our Russian friend, the Singapore coolies already are beaten with a stick. We sensed a slight fallacy in the argument again at this point, wondering whether he who was beaten was not more Christian than he who held the stick, and less diabolist than he who held such theories about those who were outside his religion. But we knew our Dostoieffsky too well to imagine that opposition can have any other effect upon a philosophic Russian than that of unloosing fresh torrents of words.

Waiting the propitious moment we rose and departed from our Russian mentor in perfect friendliness. And with Benkoolen we did the same.

Chapter Thirty Three

In Central Sumatra

FROM Benkoolen to the middle of the west coast of Sumatra there is no connection over land, but it is a fascinating sea-trip, and we followed the coast jewelled with little green islands down to Padang. At our left the blue sea stretched, broken only by the tiny islands which dotted it here and there like bunches of green palms, delicate as though they were afloat upon the blue of the water.

The little places of Padang, Fort de Kock and Padang Pandyang have but few attractions for the traveller, but the Padang Highlands, with their undulating uplands crowned by two volcanoes, are the lure. Here is the famous Karbouwen-gat, a wide valley with vertical sides, at the bottom of which the land lies flat and which offers as fine a view from any point at the top as from the bed of the valley. The land is covered with exquisitely shaped houses and rice sheds with graceful concave roof lines which are reflected in the quiet waters of fishponds. Quiet, clear water snares the blue of the sky. How glad is a Dutchman to see it again, and what nostalgia it evokes for his own flat lands of canals, lakes and quiet rivers. Almost all the inland water we have seen has been yellowish, muddy brooklets pouring down the mountains with their load of dissolved clay.

Here, however, the high roof of a mosque is repeated unbroken in the rippleless mirror of water, and pious women in white prayer garb kneel or bow their heads in the direction where the Grave of the Prophet lies. The long, tight chemises hanging to the knee, which they would otherwise wear, are brightly coloured, and it is a delight to see a procession of women going to the market place. Their stately demeanour is accentuated in this district by the long scarf, which, worn over the head and hanging down the back, causes the

" Sumatra " *(Oil painting)*

In Central Sumatra

figure to appear more slender. The same beauty of bearing is characteristic of Bali where the torso is left uncovered. It stands in strange contrast to the Palembang district or the Principalities in Java where heavy loads are carried on the bent back by leather or cotton straps across the shoulders or stretched over the forehead. Down through the valley pass the slow, heavily moving ox-carts drawn by white Indian oxen or mud-grey buffalos, carbow, as the natives call them. Leisurely they descend from the eternal solitude of the hills guided by the black ropes of palm fibre in the hands of drivers as tranquil as the beasts themselves.

The houses . . . alas! they have lost much of their earlier charm. The beautifully curved roof is but too often nowadays made of corrugated iron instead of the traditional palm leaves. It may be hygienically an advantage, but in the fierce glare of the sunlight it is a discordant note amid the harmonious hills, and only the evening light can soften its crudity. Many of the older houses, however, still retain the exquisitely carved walls, richly gilt on red, although, alas again, modern life even among the natives in this tropic remoteness is becoming too feverish to allow them time and concentration for such elaborate work.

The countryside around here is charming: lakes, brooklets, waterfalls, rocks, moss-grown and green-garlanded, give loveliness to the neighbourhood.

Then we go farther north again. By automobile this time up towards Siboga. Gradually during the three full days of our drive the hills grow wilder and more barren, and culminate at last in the imposing Devil's Land. Gigantic blocks of rock and stone lie as though the earth had been torn asunder in some primeval spasm and had thrown forth these mountainous piles; elsewhere it looks as if it had been dashed to pieces and the very rocks lie like tortured bodies distorted with pain.

This is the prelude to the mighty plain of the Batak races. If the lands we pass have fought the terrible battle of creation it is here as though their breathing still comes heavily from that struggle. Enormous *puissance* is, as it were, petrified in this heroic upland. The fields are empty. In the great swell of this very ocean of earth trees seem but shrubs. There is a little spot of darker green on a distant ridge. It proves to be a village protected by trees, but from

An Artist in the Tropics

where we stand it might be a little bush. Immensity surges about it. Slowly our eyes find the outlines of the solitary, mighty volcanoes. Yonder rises Mount Piso Piso, Mount Sibayak with its wounded sides from which the sulphur vapours eternally stream forth; Mount Sinaboong.

It is the Land of the Deluge, left untrodden since. Nothing stirs, nothing breaks the immense silence, nothing shows across its ever-undulating ridges, save the one narrow strip winding around the slopes—the road over which our automobile rushes forward. After a full day's fast journeying the masses break away to reveal the shining waters of Lake Toba, as big as a province, mysteriously distant and merged against the horizon, above which farther hills rise over banks of mist. Ever farther north we whirl in Occidental haste.

The white oxen of a convoy of carts, resting unharnessed by the side of the road, look after us with the quietude of the centuries in their dull and dreaming eyes.

A Chinese Festival (*Etching*)

Chapter Thirty Four

A Chinese Festival

BANG! Bang!! Bang! Bang!! The whole day long, near and far, the beating of drums and gongs had continued. Since it had not come within sight we had assumed that it was no more than the usual advertisement for a kinema in the adequate way peculiar to these islands, or some kind of Chinese fun. When at dusk we went out for a stroll, the insistent sound had its way with our curiosity and we were drawn to the hubbub of noise, the whirl of the crowds of which this mighty drumming formed a vortex.

The direction was indicated by the stream of people moving towards the Chinese quarter. More and more dense the throng of natives became, heavier and heavier the gongs, until at last we realised that a great festival was being celebrated. Suddenly around a corner of a street the surprise awaited us. An enormous dragon's head moved above the crowd, shaking grimly, turning furiously in all directions; then suddenly swept down and swung again into the air high above the yellow faces lifted up towards it. The dragon's illuminated eyes rolled, its lids moved up and down, its curved tongue licked voraciously along its fierce, painted jaws.

Slowly we advanced, and passing through the crowd we arrived at the square where the performance was taking place. Nearer, we saw how the dragon was given its stature on a real tower of Chinese: eight of them on the ground carried four more on their shoulders, these had two on theirs again, and the whole column was crowned by one acrobat who manipulated the dragon's head, made it turn and wheel in skilful, endless variety of movement, made it snap at a little flag which teased it from an upper window and narrowly escaped its gaping jaws.

We did not stand for very long. Out of a large shop before which everything seemed to be taking place a bowing, courteous

157

An Artist in the Tropics

Chinese came towards us and invited us to come in and take two of the seats which he had in readiness to witness the performance. Many Europeans were already seated there, and whether we wished or not, we felt constrained to accept the invitation, to join them on the little platform. So we found ourselves seated in comfortable cane chairs, provided with paper fans, and partaking of the foaming champagne and cooled lemonade which together with cigars our host provided in festival exuberance.

In the meantime the now wearied dragon descended from its exalted position, but borne by fresh men it showed a last burst of vitality as it wheeled and leaped, crawled or suddenly snapped its wide jaws in its progress around the open space. Long waved its tail, decorated by yellow and red fabrics cut into points which floated over the backs of the men beneath it. To the accompaniment of a ferocious beating of drums the monster went slower and slower; more and more the eyelids closed over the protruding eyeballs, the flaming tongue relaxed inside the mouth, and its threatening muzzle closed for the last time. Then the arena was given over to sword fighters. With fierce, staring eyes, yellow torsos bare, they performed their noble game, bowed and stretched the muscular arms, and flew like demons of a dream towards each other with short thrusts of swords or the wide swing of long lances. Then just as suddenly their performance ended.

From afar a second dragon drew near, high above the heads of the crowd, swaying as it came, its long body transparent because of the lights inside which made a marvellous interplay of light of each quaint convolution. The whimsical beast seemed indeed to be conjured by black magic to ride the air.

Its coming gave the signal for the first crash of fireworks, and in a moment there came the whole artillery of the display: the banging of heavier explosives, sparks, rays of coloured fire, showering stars, and ever and anon a swift darting arrow of fire tearing the air with a sudden hard glare. Soon a bluish haze hung everywhere, making the lights look yet more fantastic; handfuls of crackers were thrown down and ever more and more hands snatched at them. The blue smoke became thicker and floated into the shop; its irritation made the whole audience cough and their eyes water until it became unbearable and everybody fled as it were before some evil spirits bearing down upon us from behind the fusillade of the fireworks.

" CHINESE SHOPS "

A Chinese Festival

From its central square the festival broke and swept through the town. Even the music with its clanging cymbals and little drums drew away. The people surged across the arena, filled and flooded it and sauntered with laughter and babble of sound through the streets. We had taken our leave of our generous hosts at the shop, but the feast was still with us. Along the narrow turnings of the quarter the liveliness was in full swing, and the innumerable lights of the little lamps reflected in the bottles in the lemonade booths filled them with rubies. Gaily bedizened Chinese were everywhere; they had black moustaches pasted on their lips, and caps of heavy Astrakhan fur. They arranged droll processions, and bore on their arms lightly-veiled ladies as fragile and doll-like as though they were of porcelain. High above the hubbub rose the enormous trees, spreading their dark quietude above this busy frenzy and feasting

We turned a corner; the world fell still and empty. The houses were black and closed, only one was lighted by dark-red and gold lanterns. The moonlight patterned the pale walls and made a carmine glow on the closed, faint red door. Some vague light of lanterns warmed the lower part of the gable and splashed down upon the stairs which were solemn as the entrance of a temple. Silent and bent as some old watchman, the shadow of a heavy tree leaned against the clear wall, which seemed itself to slumber in the violet-coloured light.

One short scene acted as epilogue to the feast. Before the shop where we had been entertained the well-to-do proprietors were idling quietly; across the square a balcony was faintly lighted, and remote in its quiet glow showed a few graceful forms of women richly garbed in exquisite silk jackets, with costly ear-drops and glittering pins in their black hair, they moved calmly, discreetly as became ladies of rank. They had looked down on the bustling, teeming crowd, the dragons, the swordsmen. Too exalted to mix with this populous life of the streets, they had yet had their own part as spectators of the festival; nay, more, for every now and again a little flame crept into being among them, threw a pink glow over the milk-white powdered faces, and lighted up the gracefully moving hand as it threw some miniature firework, slightly crackling, down into the street. With jewelled fire and a tiny chirrup of sound their fireworks spent themselves in mid-air, dropping only an empty, coloured sheath among the crowds for which they also were too ethereal.

Chapter Thirty Five

Medan and the Batak Lands

THE impression of rubber-studded soles on the white innerside of the wooden balustrade, its outside being time-worn yellow and faint red; pink to beige-coloured walls panelled by grey woodwork; an ornamental band of black, itself adorned by white little eyes; a brown beam with bright yellow edges; a sea-green, sloping ceiling of metal plates; a white cupboard on tall legs with bottle glass doors and a little fence along the top; all this constitutes the salient features of the front verandah of our room at the hotel at Medan, the Dutch imitation of Singapore, which is itself an imitation of . . . but that inquiry would lead us too far. The front verandah is our theme, and we have far from exhausted it, neither have we enumerated its manifold blessings.

Two well-fed ladies in gilt frames look down upon us from right and left; they have white draperies wound as garlands around their resplendent persons. One is vasiform and has a white dove on her hand at which she gazes tenderly; the other equally pure, but concentrates her beatific ecstasy upon a bunch of paper flowers over her head. In their detached meditation they seem to mock at our hasty telephone-ridden existence, which attitude is consistently supported by a clock that will not go. Three so-called Japanese plates—blue, black and rose-coloured, sugared with grains of white and purple—also adorn the wall, and are aided by a sunset red and yellow as a bisected carrot, gleaming across a landscape of snow with an indecisive deer. Its companion piece is an autumn wood with birches along a brooklet. Both have green frames and grey mounts which harmonise happily with a chocolate-coloured frame wherein is displayed first a broken glass, and beyond, an English engraving, a charming landscape where ducks swim pleasantly in a pond as they are wont to do in most English landscapes. It is mouldy to

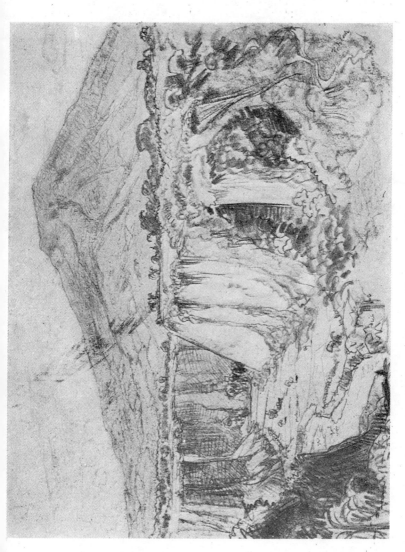

A Valley, Padang Highlands *(Drawing)*

Medan and the Batak Lands

a degree; a faint hue of woe has enveloped the scene and made it as pathetic as the dear, if humid, eyes, of the ladies of the dove and flowers. In the room one still notices the influence of so much loveliness. No impious hand has dared disturb the remembrance of a previous occupant which is kept alive by a hair-pin in the wall, just as that of an earlier one is immortalised by the piece of soap of granite-like consistency which he bequeathed to the bathroom. Little wonder, then, that we are lost in meditation and see in our mind's eye the generations who have made the dirt marks on the wall, the pillow-slips and the washstand. Not all of them have been so gentle in their sojourning. One has wrested the knob from a door; another, or mayhap, the very same, has drawn a large portion of the electric piping from the wall together with the switch. At least we begin to understand why the terms are so high for the occupation of this room, no plain hotel room, no living box for a few nights and days, but a fragrant casket of memories.

Medan is to Sumatra what Singapore is to the Malay States. It is the metropolis of planter's land. Medan boasts an English aspect since the Dutch over-estimate things foreign with all the enthusiasm that the British over-estimate things native. Medan consists of some shops, some lanes of living houses of well-to-do appearance, and above all, of our hotel, the summit and crown of mundane refinement. Here the best people come each fortnight (hari besar, the great day, it is rightly called). They forgather from the rubber and other estates to divert themselves to the accompaniment of a Jazz band. Generally this strenuous amusement is carried on until about two in the morning, but if it happens that the market price of, let us say, tobacco has exceeded expectations, this energy is displayed for a few more hours. The device is painted on the wall in suitable Gothic lettering, proclaims:

> "Wein und Weiber sind auf Erden
> Aller Weisen Hochgenusz,
> Denn sie lassen selig werden
> Ohne dass man sterben muss."

Also, on Saturdays and Sundays music is provided. This means that apart from the usual band some little lady yells English ballads à la Singapore, having instead of a dress a white satin

An Artist in the Tropics

combination costume which starts late and ends early upon her provocative person and which has black ribbons tying the legs to the wrists. The phenomenon is announced in the hall thus:

To-day:
Salmon.
Turbot.
Rita Field.

The music plays a perfect avalanche of English music hall stuff and then "Komm, Schatz, wir trinken ein Likörchen" ("Come, dear, let's have a liqueur"), and "Rosalie, Fleck am Knie" as carefully stated on the menu. Everybody will realise that Medan sees life with cosmopolitan verve.

It is generally thought that men work more intensely in the East Indies than in Europe; were it not so said a sober visitor might deduce it from the intensity of their repose in these interstices of labour. Certainly the isolation on the estates is even worse here than in Java, and the reaction from this yields the outburst in Medan each fortnight. At least Deli, as this part of Sumatra is called, has a great variety of day-off amusement lore. The piano which was flung overboard as a protest against the musical efforts of a persistent player, and which was replaced by a cheque, is one of the sagas in Deli's mythology. Others are: the Lighted Furniture of the Club-house, the Chandelier Bombarded with Chairs, the Race of Two Driverless Motor Cars up the Clubhouse Stairs, this as a preliminary hill-climbing test, and . . . but the rest of the list may be heard almost any day of Hari Besar, the Great, Great Day. When fortunes are in the crucible the temperature is high.

In the neighbourhood lies Brastagi among the cooler hills. If Medan is the London, the Paris of the district, this is the Brighton, the Plage. Chiefly the Brighton, for it is most patronised by the English from the Straits Settlements. They don a dinner jacket— the national symbol of homage to food—in honour of the gramophone and fox trot. This finished they take to sports or on occasions make a trip to the Volcano Sibayak. Ceaselessly it pours forth its steam; the lands quiver in the glare of the sun, and beyond the field of vision lie the lonely estates. Here is no Jazz, no smoking jacket, no gramophone. All that has penetrated to these wild, primitive

The Batak High Plain   (Drawing)

Medan and the Batak Lands

lands and their inhabitants, the Batak people, from Western culture may be said in two words—sewing-machine and umbrella.

The often half-naked Bataks, going about as beasts of the field in their natural simplicity, yet have a real passion for our awful black umbrella. Rough fellows, sometimes with a cap of hurdlework on their heads which compares best to a frayed, torn fig-basket, with cannibalism hardly a step behind them, love to add to their toilet the absurd and fundamentally unnecessary umbrella. The most striking way of carrying it to our view was that of having it lying horizontally on the head whilst the almost naked owner strode beneath it undisturbed. Perhaps he considers it a sign of dignity as some suppose that the missionaries, who are very active in this region, have unconsciously made it a symbol of godliness and good behaviour.

This theory, however, does not hold with the other offspring of European culture among the Batak tribes, but there can be little doubt that the sewing-machine is to more practical purpose in their existences. The women weave their sombre or lightly-coloured materials in simple but extremely harmonious designs with that innate taste which cannot but impress the European as belonging to any race in the East whose decorative feeling has remained unspoiled by the Occidental factory stuff.

The Batak villages are still surrounded by thick walls, although these serve no longer as fortresses against the inhabitants of the next village since the Dutch stamped out the looting and head-hunting expeditions among them. These walls of immense, high-piled blocks of rock are mostly overgrown, but still have the narrow entrances easily closed in case of emergency. The large houses, in each of which several families live, stand in straight rows. Like the rice-sheds and most buildings, they stand on high poles to prevent the entrance of the animals, but also to render them inaccessible to men when the long bamboo ladder is withdrawn. Windows are unknown to the Batak; a single door is all there is.

Cleanliness is not an obvious Batak virtue for these reasons; more so as under the living house the swine are fenced in and water is rare in the wild, high lands. From a single well many women bring home the necessary water for their families in bamboo tubes always carried horizontally on the head, however mountainous the ground may be.

The sides of a Batak house, a fine wooden structure, lean out like the sides of a vessel, and carry a tremendous roof with ridge-ends

An Artist in the Tropics

crowned by horned heads which will keep away the evil spirits. As a genuine Polynesian, the Batak ties the planks of his house together with the black rope made from palm fibre, and he invariably makes a fine ornament of them, taking the crocodile's head as motive.

Women weave, women sweep the village yard, dye the threads, carry goods to market, and fetch the water. Women are the beasts of burden. A sinister procession they form with their great loads on their heads carrying two or three children on their backs, as they proceed to the market-place in hundreds. Often they have all imaginable distortions caused by their rough labouring. They file away the teeth and chew the red, juicy "sirih", walk through mud and bushes clothed in rags and covered with dust.

The Batak men do not work. In the old days they went out fighting and hunting, and have not yet found other employment than gossip and chess. Work has no attraction, and even the women do not like the men to work for money. Adonia, as our christened boy at the hotel is called, would like to marry, but among these tropical buccaneers women disdain a hotel servant. A man should fight or do nothing; play chess as a substitute if need be. Moreover marriage is a costly business. In the old days £5 or £8 of Dutch money was an adequate sum to offer to the family as dowry, but since prices have risen this will no longer suffice and something like £20 is demanded.

Under the stress of necessity the Batak man will work, but no regular employment will hold him. Little wonder that the estates of Northern Sumatra, dependent as they are upon careful and regular labour, unable to dispense with intense and systematic culture, import their hands. Thus Deli is a mixture of races: Chinese abound, Japanese have come across of recent years, martial Sikhs are guards, long bearded men from British India sit in the streets, and when their naturally long beard proves troublesome in this new world they split it in two, take up the ends and twist them into the hair at the chin again. Past them, with clean-shaven, sly faces, go the Chettys, who have from time immemorial been the usurers and money-changers here. Almost black and naked Klingalese work like ancient demons, their tendinous arms and legs ceaselessly active, at the great pots of asphalt; slave at the making of the very modern road along which the slow ox-carts and swift automobiles go fraternally side by side.

Houses in the Padang Highlands *(Drawing)*

Chapter Thirty Six

Piso   Piso

WHAT Fridolin, the cook, prepares is brought to our room by Adonia, and if this young man is busy in the dining-room Bismarck carries it in for us.

Victims of malaria we are. We lie here at the large Lake Toba and have our meals in the room of the small hotel which has been put down, just simply put down, on the waste and empty chaos of the Batak High Plain.

Soft steps of bare feet. A little cough, "Khm!" on the front verandah.

"Come in, Bismarck," I shout from my bed.

Silence.

Another little cough, "Khm!"

Bismarck does not dare very much.

Again I shout, but it is no use. I slip out of bed and open the door, and here he comes, our own darling little Bismarck, hesitatingly and shyly, with his big tray very carefully balanced. He is about twelve years old, we guess, and he does his best. We wonder whether he would himself know whom he is called after, and whether Pepin, the plate-washer, has any notion of the royal origin of his name. The naïve Batak seems as fond of a European name as a wild negro of a pocket mirror.

The Rhine mission is especially operative here, and it scatters romantic and operatic names around the district, and there must be a charm, we ponder, and certainly a profound difference, to have been a cannibal once and now to be converted, baptised, and a Christian just as good as the Tuan himself, with a name from romantic literature to symbolise the change.

What's in a name? To the Batak a great deal, no doubt. The question arises whether the desire for nomenclature does not play a material part in the conversion. We may be mistaken, but there is something embarrassing in having a number of Bismarcks and Pepins to attend to one. We have once read that the Spaniards in Mexico under Cortez worked on more wholesale lines when they had large numbers to be converted. The first day they baptised from morning until nightfall every native entered the fold of grace under the name of Pedro. The second day gave every fellow the name of Juan; the third, Roderigo; and so forth. A practical solution—one had almost said American—and with the advantage that no name with a very personal significance would descend upon someone so unlike his namesake as was our gentle little Bismarck to the German Chancellor. "Kareta-Api", which is fire-waggon, and the Malay for railway carriage, is the name of a baby born in a train, which occasionally happens to these natural, simply living children of the soil. Some, we have been told, get the name of some firm of preserve manufacturers, as these are abundantly used out in the East by Europeans. The name on the tin being so profusely spread must doubtless seem to the native very Christian and worthy of perpetuation We have not personally met any native so called, and regret that we cannot record a conversation between a Lea-and-Perrin and a Cross-and-Blackwell.

The value of the conversion, in so far as it has helped to put an end to cannibalism, is beyond dispute. Also much has been done for general health conditions. A large nursing home was built for lepers, and all praise is due to the missionaries who devote their lives to such work. But the real aim of conversion, one would imagine, is more than this, and whether the Batak really does benefit beyond getting his excellent name is to us, at least, a moot point. We occasionally wondered as we travelled in the East whether the missionaries might not devote a deal of attention to the remoulding of certain Christians, who seemed not to demonstrate Christian principles with any great emphasis. We have even thought at times that charity might begin at home.

But this is mere theory. The Western mind, with its pride in logic, is far less logical than that of the Oriental. The Western mind, anxious to organise, settle and arrange all sorts of business which rightly concerns somebody else, is lost in business. Since we are Dutch ourselves we have a right to say that the Dutch are very Occidental in this respect. The Oriental mind is satisfied with

BANKS OF LAKE TOBA (*Drawing*)

Piso Piso

itself entirely: the mind is lost in the mind. There is danger and advantages in both viewpoints, but the understanding of each by each is not easily attained.

To return to Piso Piso! We are in the kindly care of the hotel manager and his wife, who do everything possible for us. It is a real relief, and we have also a very reliable doctor, who visits us despite the difficulty of having to travel for over two hours through wild country to reach us. If a thunderstorm is in the air—a daily occurrence here, high among the clouds—you cannot use the telephone to ask him to come. Nevertheless the situation has its compensations, for we have been sent here by our previous doctor down in Medan, and in consequence have got rid of him. The good man has been treating us for about a month for influenza; he has made no suggestion that it might be malaria. To recuperate after his influenza we were sent to the cool air here in the mountains, and forthwith the fever began again. The second doctor came and immediately diagnosed malaria. Through his microscope we were shown our own parasites, and had it explained how long we had given them hospitality under the cloak of influenza.

We were a little amazed about our first doctor practising in such a medical centre as Medan is. Had we but known the second attack which threatened we would certainly not have allowed ourselves to be sent to such an out-of-the-way health resort as this, so far from medicine and Æsculapius, and as unpractical as it is costly. But when later we recounted indignantly this experience, nobody seemed surprised. It seemed almost the usual treatment of a patient, and we revealed our ignorance of Eastern usage by any such astonishment at local medical intelligence. Only one month of wrong treatment! Our interrogators would indicate our good fortune and assure us that we should know better what to expect after a year in the East. Later on we did learn the lesson, for when after some time we again fell ill in Java, the doctor stated that it "did not mean anything" and that in two days we should be well again, gave us medicine and disappeared. We were ill for three weeks instead of his two days, and before we left the town we stumbled to his house to pay the bill.

"What, have the potions not helped you? Why, it must have been something else, then," remarked the gentleman laconically, and then, consolingly: "But you are all right again, anyway."

An Artist in the Tropics

We go, and thank Heaven; but consider whether in future it would not be wiser to look at the payment of such bills with equal inconsequence.

It was distressing to be forced so much against our wills to postpone concerts. Neither the patients nor the committees enjoyed the change of plans, and among these latter some assumed at once that this was another of the eternal poses of these artist people, and others wrote registered letters with almost indecent haste to cancel the engagement.

A pity, we would decide, to waste the extra stamp, and the fragments of the letter flutter like a swarm of butterflies over the wide lake. We see them sporting down the air with little grief, for our first enthusiasm is to get better, and however much Piso Piso may be at the end of the earth, there was rest there, and silence, and air which could be breathed without choking.

Some five thousand feet above the sea level we are. Round us lie scarcely populated, wide lands around the mountain after which the hotel is called. The rooms, situated in a row, all face the lake which a few thousand feet beneath lies in everlasting silence. No voice, no rumour is heard from below. From the cupola at the edge of the steep slope we have a tremendous view over the northern part of the lake, the total length of which is some sixty miles. To the left lies the Land of a Thousand Hills, Seriboo Dolok, suddenly sloping down into whimsically shaped peninsulas and tongues of land with lumpy and notched banks. To the right, the straight, high cliffs stand in strange, pale tints as of faded gobelin or antique velvet, whilst at the horizon, often wrapped in mists and so only occasionally visible, the island Samosir begins, around which the lake circles. The reddish ground is coarse, bare and unfertile as a desert.

Far beneath our feet, like some great prehistoric animal crouching at the water's edge, lies the sprawled bulk of a peninsula, empty and treeless. Nor does any vegetation cover the slopes, the Thousand Hills, the high mountains. Only the highest summits have a cap of green.

"Would the ground be too stony?" we ask the hotel proprietor, who knows the land well, having constructed a road to the place where he erected his hotel, branching off somewhere from a Government road.

Piso Piso

"You must know the Batak to understand," he says. "The trees we have planted grow quite well, but if the Batak wants to grow rice he catches fire to the high dry grass, the alang-alang, which is the height of a man and will blaze immediately. Thus a piece of land is burnt maybe ten times the size of that which is needed; but that is of no consequence: there is ample ground and few Bataks. They have hardly anything to do to the rice. As water is rare they cannot as a rule here grow rice on the wet fields, the 'sawahs', but leave it to itself on the dry 'ladang'. The harvest over, the Batak will burn down a new stretch and incidentally destroy the bushes and young trees which have grown up in the meantime. I often see it. The trees which the population need to shadow their houses grow well enough, as they take care to spare these. But you will see fires in the enormous lands before you almost every day."

So indeed it is. As though Titans were making offerings to their gods, day after day great columns of smoke rise up from the old, ever-silent lands, as they have risen for ages and ages.

Every day the lake is there, but every day it is different. Only the great silence is eternal, enveloping the immensity of the land as by enchantment—the world before man came it seems. All these vague, transparent and remote colourings have something unreal in them, and nothing familiar can the eye distinguish. No human form could be visible from the height where we stand. A tiny mark on the water, which might be a drifting piece of wood, reveals itself through the glasses as a proa with twenty men aboard. A few stones at the water's edge? The telescope changes them into a herd of buffaloes bathing. No sound, no movement.

But ever the water changes. Now it is blue and purplish, like mother-of-pearl, varying to green as it nears the coast. Strange curving lines have been drawn by the currents on its surface as though it were marble. On another day we think we can distinguish the glitter of the sun on the deep blue, but what we see are the white tops of great waves, though neither wind nor movement is perceptible from where we stand. Perhaps a heavy cloud will pass across, vanish mysteriously as a ghost as it comes into contact with forces unsensed by us; or another will roll down the hillside and spread over the entire surface of the water, hiding the island. Suddenly a squall will beat up the water to a foaming mass, torment it wildly, blow it to spume and dig great whirlpools—from our height we

An Artist in the Tropics

hardly see a ripple. When on another occasion the face of the water is strangely striped the Batak will tell you that what you see is the great snake which lives beneath the lake, and that if it moves, storm is on the water, earthquake and mishap will occur.

Beyond our horizon again the highlands are the home of the steppe-men; dark is their look, dark their skin, dark their indigo-coloured garb.

In the afternoons storm-laden cumuli, which all day have hung like heavy garlands around the mountain tops, spread down over the land. Curiously their rolling movement eclipses the land. Heavy skies clamber down from the throne which Mount Piso Piso has been; vision is blotted out, everything is clad in grey, all colour fades behind a grey mist of rain which hangs like some transparent curtain close about us. After the showers have gone this land-in-the-clouds is still enveloped in a white moisture such as Matthew Maris dreamed in his art.

OX-CART AT LAKE TOBA (*Oil painting*)

Chapter Thirty Seven

Singapore

SINGAPORE to the non-commercial, non-political, non-nautical visitor is mainly a rickshaw.

Twelve thousand of them they have there.

Need one define a rickshaw, that light carriage with two wheels, the taxi-cab of the East, wherein you go to your destination pulled by—a human creature, in so far as the Chinese coolie counts as such? Twelve thousand rickshaws; twelve thousand coolies.

They go barefooted at a trot. Barefooted all Orientals go, but it is a strange feeling when for the first time you step into the rickshaw, your coolie lifts the shafts, and . . . plop! you fall backwards and the fellow has run away with you before you know what has happened. A hat and short trousers, sometimes a linen jacket are all he is wearing, with occasionally a rag round his neck to dry the perspiration. The coolies only speak Chinese, which no traveller knows. But it does not matter. If you wish to turn left you pat them on some left hand projection of their anatomy, which is much more effective than mentioning direction or destination, for this will only prompt their one English word "yes" and your coolie will dash off with you to Heaven knows where and indicate by a reassuring grimace that this is really the place you have demanded. We have often appreciated the coolies' temptation in the matter, but probably not many travellers can imagine themselves and their own mental reactions if Fate had placed them between the shafts of a rickshaw. Automatically the coolie overcharges. Automatically one takes no notice. The police have fixed a reasonable tariff, but so arbitrary a thing has never familiarised itself in the Oriental mind.

To the newcomer there is a curious novelty in the idea of a man running about with you in the tropical heat in order that you

An Artist in the Tropics

yourself may remain cool. Here it is so common that you cannot walk undisturbed. Nobody but a rickshaw coolie goes on foot and perspires correspondingly. There is no road where rickshaw men are not waiting. One will be chewing like a man-ape on a huge piece of sugar cane a yard long. When he no longer wants one piece in his mouth he will open his jaws cavernously and it will fall down somewhere. Another lies asleep in his carriage. Your foot-plank is his cushion, and it is certainly no harder than the stone which would serve him for pillow in his native land, where no protecting tariff would assure justice to his waking hours and consequent peace to his dreams.

The Occidental looks after tariffs, trying honestly to be just. Have we not read this very morning in *The Straits Times* that an English official was put in prison because he had abused the trust put in him by a Chinese and Malay? Does not Baedeker say it himself: "If the improbable disaster befell the land that the beneficial and just English Government came to an end to-day, despotism would be established to-morrow."

And if the coolies run, many of them with monstrously swollen calves, and varicose veins as thick as one's finger sometimes, in China itself they would do the same and risk dying of hunger, all twelve thousand of them, without anybody having the faintest regard for their death. We realise that these Chinese are not the pick of the basket. Their corruption must be great, but with all their coarseness these men have a hereditary culture which our dockers and unskilled labourers might well envy. We, at any rate, were glad to be able to obtain a little bowl from which we had seen a rickshaw man eat his sober meal, having succeeded in explaining our desire in language of gesture to the equal satisfaction of both parties. It now stands on a cupboard as the fine thing which it is.

Singapore itself is a port, more a harbour than a town. Constantly the steamers come and go, flying all flags, displaying all shapes. Commerce, business, money-interests, the fox-trot and the gramophone are its whole alphabet. More charm and beauty dwell in the Chinese quarter, though the smells there are somewhat disconcerting. But when a little note is made in a sketch book, an interested, distinguished Chinese invites us to inspect the inside of his house as well. He shows us the altar where the tablets of his ancestors are honoured, the beautifully written scripts on the walls,

Singapore

the cool, green inner-court with trees carefully arranged. The whole lovely house was brimmed with silence which made us feel that we had penetrated the innermost places of China itself.

Yonder in the harbour the steam whistles scream continually, and the haste of the modern Occidental world tears through the days. But alongside it all an ancient Chinese junk floats like some strange beast of the waters, secretly, the high notched sails ribbed like a dragon's wing; and an enchantment hovers about it, such as would cling to some fragile shell from a sunken land of fairies strangely brought forth from the sea.

Chapter Thirty Eight

Malta

"WELL, Mr. Paderewski, are you going ashore too?" we ask our Polish fellow passenger, who is leaning over the rail with us. His name is not exactly Paderewski, but as it is unpronounceable to the majority on board, that of the famous pianist has been thrust upon him.

Soon a brilliantly-coloured rowing boat brings us to the coast, without Mr. Paderewksi, who prefers an afternoon siesta, and immediately we are in Italy. Baskets full of sunny oranges, vegetables, flowers, are gaily displayed. Old-fashioned black carriages, with four little black curtains along black pillars carrying the roof, with black horses, supplant the rickshaw to which we have become accustomed, but they are too funereal to tempt one in this glorious, and at last amiable sunshine of the Mediterranean. We go on foot, and climb the long stairway of the street to the main square.

Here the women again have rosy, pink-coloured faces, showing brightly against their black wide head-dresses or scarves. The yellowish or pale orange houses scintillate in the gay light, and the sky is of a deep, southern blue, the atmosphere, the sea air, so stimulating and refreshing that one hardly notices the lack of trees.

How delightfully Italian this Italy is! A herd of sheep jostle through the main street, though British men-of-war lie in the harbour. Here is the enormous church, as one finds enormous churches at every turn in Italy. We turn inside.

As the heavy doors close down upon us, and we, still blinded by the bright glare of the sun and the old, but ever-young, sea, can barely distinguish the gilt arches in front of us, a ghost shuffles hastily towards us on slippered feet from the darkness, and before

176

Malta

vision has revealed to us a yellow, withered face with a white beard, the ancient muttering of a strange accent begins to flow unstaunchably to our ears.

"The floor is all marble—white marble from Carrara and yellow marble from Piacenza, laid in 1653 by Giacomo Mirandabella, who died in 1687." We try to escape this learned-by-rote wisdom with its trickle of meaningless dates which seem to have such a strange fascination for the British tourists, however little they appeal to self-respecting Dutchmen, who do not share this mania for quasi-historical detail; but he pursues us with more. "The Altar by Antonio da San Falla, 1753, and the marble statues by Tarantazzini, who died in Rome in 1681, and was a pupil of Carapatella Rizzio, the friend of . . ."

Little use is our turning here for a flying retreat. He has had too perfect a training on who knows how many Anglo-Saxons. The muttering is in full spate:

"These are the apostles by Caldara and Buonaventi, and on the other side" (this to outmanœuvre a sudden turn by us) "a painting by Michel Angelo, and . . ." but he has already noticed for the first time a gleam of interest. "Painting by Michel Angelo," he repeats continually. "Fine painting by Michel Angelo." "Even kijken?" (Have a look?) we hesitatingly ask. Of course it will be nothing; he is just drivelling, we think aloud in Dutch, and then: "Perhaps we had better look. Who knows? the thing may be genuine, and then it would be worth the trouble of looking for and of listening to the new flood of information which it will unloose."

"Through here," commands the little ghost, glad that at last he has our ears. We have not crossed the threshold of the little chapel when the unending historian recommences: "This picture is a copy from Rubens by Garcella Francia. . . ."

"Is that your Michel Angelo?"

"No, there, behind that marble group of angels. The large painting by Michel Angelo, the small one by Fratellini da Urbino. The figure in the centre represents St. John, the lady is . . ."

We are tricked. "I told you so," we blame each other, and warn our guide that his Michel Angelo may well rejoice that it is so dark there. We press an unmerited tip into his hand, and even as we escape at last his muttering follows us through the gloom of the church.

An Artist in the Tropics

" . . . the ceiling decorated by Ricardo Torrabadella and the glass windows from 1533, restored in 1846."

As we dash from his insistence we feel that the spell of the East has at last been broken. We are home again, Occidental again, deep in the European tradition, caught up the known, familiar things. Europe again. Europe again.

Some other Oxford Paperbacks for readers interested in Central Asia,
China and South-East Asia, past and present

CAMBODIA
GEORGE COEDES
Angkor

MALCOLM MacDONALD
Angkor and the Khmers*

CENTRAL ASIA
PETER FLEMING
Bayonets to Lhasa

ANDRE GUIBAUT
Tibetan Venture

LADY MACARTNEY
An English Lady in Chinese
Turkestan

DIANA SHIPTON
The Antique Land

C. P. SKRINE AND
PAMELA NIGHTINGALE
Macartney at Kashgar*

ERIC TEICHMAN
Journey to Turkistan

ALBERT VON LE COQ
Buried Treasures of Chinese
Turkestan

AITCHEN K. WU
Turkistan Tumult

CHINA
All About Shanghai: A Standard
Guide

HAROLD ACTON
Peonies and Ponies

VICKI BAUM
Shanghai '37

ERNEST BRAMAH
Kai Lung's Golden Hours*

ERNEST BRAMAH
The Wallet of Kai Lung*

ANN BRIDGE
The Ginger Griffin

CHANG HSIN-HAI
The Fabulous Concubine*

CARL CROW
Handbook for China

PETER FLEMING
The Siege at Peking

MARY HOOKER
Behind the Scenes in Peking

NEALE HUNTER
Shanghai Journal*

REGINALD F. JOHNSTON
Twilight in the Forbidden City

GEORGE N. KATES
The Years that Were Fat

CORRINNE LAMB
The Chinese Festive Board

W. SOMERSET
MAUGHAM
On a Chinese Screen*

G. E. MORRISON
An Australian in China

DESMOND NEILL
Elegant Flower

PETER QUENNELL
Superficial Journey through
Tokyo and Peking

OSBERT SITWELL
Escape with Me! An Oriental
Sketch-book

J. A. TURNER
Kwang Tung or Five Years in
South China

HONG KONG AND
MACAU
AUSTIN COATES
City of Broken Promises

AUSTIN COATES
A Macao Narrative

AUSTIN COATES
Macao and the British, 1637–1842

AUSTIN COATES
Myself a Mandarin

AUSTIN COATES
The Road

The Hong Kong Guide 1893

INDONESIA
DAVID ATTENBOROUGH
Zoo Quest for a Dragon*

VICKI BAUM
A Tale from Bali*

'BENGAL CIVILIAN'
Rambles in Java and the Straits
in 1852

MIGUEL COVARRUBIAS
Island of Bali*

AUGUSTA DE WIT
Java: Facts and Fancies

JACQUES DUMARÇAY
Borobudur

JACQUES DUMARÇAY
The Temples of Java

ANNA FORBES
Unbeaten Tracks in Islands of the
Far East

GEOFFREY GORER
Bali and Angkor

JENNIFER LINDSAY
Javanese Gamelan

EDWIN M. LOEB
Sumatra: Its History and People

MOCHTAR LUBIS
The Outlaw and Other Stories

MOCHTAR LUBIS
Twilight in Djakarta

MADELON H. LULOFS
Coolie*

MADELON H. LULOFS
Rubber

COLIN McPHEE
A House in Bali*

ERIC MJÖBERG
Forest Life and Adventures in the
Malay Archipelago

H. W. PONDER
Java Pageant

HICKMAN POWELL
The Last Paradise

F. M. SCHNITGER
Forgotten Kingdoms in Sumatra

E. R. SCIDMORE
Java, The Garden of the East

MICHAEL SMITHIES
Yogyakarta: Cultural Heart of
Indonesia

LADISLAO SZÉKELY
Tropic Fever: The Adventures of
a Planter in Sumatra

EDWARD C. VAN NESS
AND SHITA
PRAWIROHARDJO
Javanese Wayang Kulit

HARRY WILCOX
Six Moons in Sulawesi

MALAYSIA
ODOARDO BECCARI
Wanderings in the Great
Forests of Borneo

ISABELLA L. BIRD
The Golden Chersonese: Travels
in Malaya in 1879

MARGARET BROOKE
THE RANEE OF
SARAWAK
My Life in Sarawak

SIR HUGH CLIFFORD
Saleh: A Prince of Malaya

HENRI FAUCONNIER
The Soul of Malaya

W. R. GEDDES
Nine Dayak Nights

C. W. HARRISON
Illustrated Guide to the Federated
Malay States (1923)

BARBARA HARRISSON
Orang-Utan

TOM HARRISSON
Borneo Jungle

TOM HARRISSON
World Within: A Borneo Story

CHARLES HOSE
The Field-Book of a Jungle-Wallah

CHARLES HOSE
Natural Man

W. SOMERSET
MAUGHAM
Ah King and Other Stories*

W. SOMERSET
MAUGHAM
The Casuarina Tree*

MARY McMINNIES
The Flying Fox*

ROBERT PAYNE
The White Rajahs of Sarawak

CARVETH WELLS
Six Years in the Malay Jungle

SINGAPORE
RUSSELL GRENFELL
Main Fleet to Singapore

R. W. E. HARPER AND
HARRY MILLER
Singapore Mutiny

MASANOBU TSUJI
Singapore 1941–1942

G. M. REITH
Handbook to Singapore (1907)

C. E. WURTZBURG
Raffles of the Eastern Isles

THAILAND
CARL BOCK
Temples and Elephants

REGINALD CAMPBELL
Teak-Wallah

ANNA LEONOWENS
The English Governess at the
Siamese Court

MALCOLM SMITH
A Physician at the Court of Siam

ERNEST YOUNG
The Kingdom of the Yellow Robe

Titles marked with an asterisk have restricted rights.